THE CELTIC CROSS

THE CELTIC CROSS

AN ILLUSTRATED HISTORY AND CELEBRATION

NIGEL PENNICK

BLANDFORD

A BLANDFORD BOOK

First published in the UK 1997 by Blandford
A Cassell Imprint
Cassell plc, Wellington House,
125 Strand, London WC2R 0BB

First paperback edition 1998

Distributed in the United States by Sterling Publishing Co., Inc.,
387 Park Avenue South, New York, NY 10016-8810

**A Cataloguing-in-Publication Data entry for this title
is available from the British Library**

ISBN 0-7137-2758-6

Typeset by Falcon Oast Graphic Art, East Hoathly, Sussex
Printed and bound in Great Britain
by The Bath Press

CONTENTS

I dedicate this book
to my Celtic ancestors,
both from the Kingdom of Kernow
and of the Race of Diarmid.

The three principal endeavours of a Bard:
One is to learn and collect sciences,
The second is to teach,
And the third is to make peace
and to put an end to all injury;
for to do contrary to these things
is not usual or becoming to a Bard.

The Triads of Britain

PREFACE

The Celtic Cross is known throughout the world as the emblem of Celtic Christianity, and in many ways it can be considered the symbol of Celticness itself. In this book, I present an overview of the rich spiritual ground from which grew the Celtic Cross as we know it, celebrating its forerunners and the Celtic Cross itself through the diversity of historical designs and as a continuing manifestation of the living tradition of Celtic art.

Nigel Campbell Pennick
Bar Hill
Candlemas Eve 1996

AUTHOR'S NOTE: I use the terms BCE and CE to denote years 'Before the Common Era' and 'Common Era'. The terms BC (Before Christ) and AD (Anno Domini – the year of the Lord) are specifically Christian, while BCE and CE are ideologically neutral.

INTRODUCTION - THE CELTS

The Celtic tradition is one of the most recognizable elements of contemporary European culture, and it is also one of the most ancient. Celtic tradition can trace its roots back over 2,700 years. The ancient Greeks gave the barbarian peoples who lived to the north of them the name *Keltoi*. Although these central European Celts were not a genetically coherent ethnic group, or a political union, nevertheless they formed a specific, recognizable culture, with shared elements of language, religious beliefs and artistic outlook. Around 650 BCE, the Celts were influenced by Greek and Etruscan culture, and, by adding and adapting these elements to the Hallstatt culture, the characteristically Celtic style of art came into being. The first recognizably Celtic civilization emerged around 500 BCE in northeast France and the middle Rhine, which is called the 'early La Tène period', after the place where the characteristic artefacts of the period were discovered. Early in the fourth century BCE, the Celtic tribes expanded westwards into what is now France and the British Isles. They moved southwest into the Iberian peninsula, south into northern Italy and east through the Balkans into Asia Minor.

This expansion of the Celts was not permanent, for, from the first century BCE onwards, they suffered reverses. They were expelled from eastern Europe by Slavic tribes, and conquered by the Romans first in northern Italy and then in the rest of Gaul, modern Switzerland, southern Germany and Austria. In the first century CE, the Romans conquered most of Britain. In the third century CE, the Celts in southern Germany were overwhelmed by the Alamannic peoples. Today, many centuries later, despite many further historical vicissitudes, Celtic culture has not been eliminated from Europe. It has left its mark in England, France and Switzerland, parts of Austria, Germany, Hungary,

OPPOSITE: The archetypal Celtic Cross as sunwheel.

9

Spain and northern Italy, while Ireland, Wales, Scotland, Cornwall, the Isle of Man and Brittany are still predominantly Celtic in culture.

The Celts have always given great respect to the arts, especially the spoken word. In former times, the highest honours were bestowed upon the bards, and the druids taught their doctrines through the techniques of a highly developed art of memory. The Celtic worldview was non-literalistic: it was expressed through a complex series of symbols and metaphors that gave access to the invisible inner nature of things. Even when they were conquered, the Celts never lost their exceptional abilities. Under Roman rule in north Italy, Celtic families produced many outstanding men of letters in the Latin tradition, among them Cato, Catullus, Varro and Vergil. Later, in the north, Irish, British and Breton bards laid the foundations of the medieval literature of western Europe, and the tradition has continued unbroken until the present time. Celtic writers of the twentieth century have been among the most pre-eminent, among them William Butler Yeats, Dylan Thomas and Seamus Heaney. As a medium of the intellect, Celtic art crystallizes the essential infinity of the cosmos and gives expression to it in physical form.

The religion of the Celts was an integral part of the culture of everyday life, was nature-venerating, polytheistic, and recognized goddesses as well as gods, which were represented both aniconically and iconically. According to the best accounts, Pagan Celtic spirituality recognized the cyclic nature of existence, which involved reincarnation of individuals, and immediate continuity between the material world and the otherworld. The druidic teachings, which have come down to us through Welsh tradition, tell of an integrated relationship between humans and nature, expressed through a vast body of natural lore concerning the seasons, the stars, matter and existence. Celtic spirituality has always recognized that there is an unseen world that interpenetrates the visible world. Everything exists on several simultaneous levels: human consciousness interprets them as the physical, the spiritual and the symbolic. Celtic religion understood the course of nature as the will of the Gods. In accordance with this, they venerated both local and general deities, which they saw as being present in natural sanctuaries, especially in ensouled places in the landscape. So their main places of worship were at holy hills, springs, rivers, lakes, trees and in woodland. Thus, Celtic culture was integrated with nature, expressed through the multiple possibilities of life itself. Most of this traditional lore is still known and preserved in Celtic folk-tradition.

1

THE HISTORICAL BACKGROUND OF THE CELTIC CROSS

Unlike southern Britain, Ireland and most of what is now Scotland were never incorporated into the Roman Empire. Consequently, the traditions of the late Iron Age, which had come to an end in the rest of the Celtic realms, continued to develop. Classical Graeco-Roman art had transformed the sacred arts in Celtic parts of the empire, but it had relatively little impact in Ireland and northern Britain. There, the ancient Celtic art was perpetuated and developed along its own lines. In Ireland, the Pagan Celtic religion also continued in a form which had ceased elsewhere. In its forms and style, Irish religion was paralleled further east by the Pagan religions of the Germans, Scandinavians, Slavs and Balts, but in Britain and Gaul Romanization had significantly altered Paganism. In Ireland and Pictland, the Pagan Celtic religion continued in an older form which had ceased elsewhere, for druidry flourished in Ireland long after the Romans had extirpated it in Britain. The Celtic pantheon, too, was revered by the Picts and Irish in a wholly Celtic manner, while in Britain and Gaul it had been incorporated into Roman religion. By means of the *interpretatio Romana*, the Romans identified indigenous goddesses and gods with their nearest parallel in the Roman pantheon, thereby adding a Roman element to all of the indigenous religions within the Empire.

The Romanization of southern Britain also meant that elements of middle eastern religions were introduced there in the shape of the worship of Cybele, Attis, Isis, Sekhmet, Serapis, Mithras, Jupiter Dolichenus and Jesus Christ. Thus in Ireland, unlike in Britain, there was a direct transition from druidism to Christianity without the intermediate stage of Romanization. This is the reason why Ireland saw the creation of a specific type of religion, Celtic Christianity.

Towards the end of the western Roman empire, the Christian religion had entered Britain, but it was a minority interest, and society on the whole remained pluralistic, with Christianity remaining one cult among many. Even after the Emperor in Constantinople made Christianity the state religion, Paganism retained a significant role in Britain, far from the imperial centre. In the middle of the fourth century, for example, when the Empire was officially Christian, the Pagan temple at Verulamium (St Albans) was reconstructed, and the therapeutic shrine of Mars Nodens at Lydney in Gloucestershire was expanded greatly. Also at this time, at Cirencester, the Roman governor of South Britain restored the Jupiter Column, one of the forerunners of the Celtic Cross. Only after the withdrawal of the Roman military in the year 410 did Christian missionaries make inroads into much of Britain. *The Lives of the British Saints* (Honourable Society of Cymmrodorion, 1908) shows that most of them preached and converted in the fifth, sixth and seventh centuries.

The Romanization of southern Britain also meant that elements of middle eastern religions were introduced there in the shape of the worship of Cybele, Attis, Isis, Sekhmet, Serapis, Mithras, Jupiter Dolichenus and Jesus Christ.

CHRISTIAN MONASTICISM AND THE CELTIC CHURCH

Christian monasticism arose in the deserts of Egypt and Syria. Either to escape persecution, or to flee from the follies of the world, some Christian priests became ascetics, and went to live in remote desert retreats, far from civilization. Seeking spiritual perfection, they adopted the ascetic traditions of the priests of the Hellenized Egyptian deities Isis and Serapis, copying some of their customs, such as shaving the head in a tonsure. Even the practice of living together in monasteries was taken from Isian tradition. By entering the desert with virtually no possessions, the Christian monks effected their escape from what they saw as a decadent and corrupt society, so that they could create a new, independent religious way. Their ultimate objective was the recreation of Paradise through the reunification of body and spirit. This was to be accomplished by re-establishing the human body as a point of contact between heaven and earth. The fathers of this 'school', St Paul of Thebes and St Anthony of Egypt, viewed what they saw as the fallen state of human beings as an aberration from their natural state of grace. Through the resolution of disharmony, they argued, human beings could regain balance and wellbeing and return to their true condition as the image and likeness of God. Then, the unnatural separation between the physical and the spiritual world would be at an end.

However, this reunion of the human with the divine did not entail a war against nature, which they recognized as the perfect manifestation of God's creation. So, when a visiting philosopher asked St Anthony how he could survive intellectually in the desert without the scriptures, the saint gestured towards the landscape and answered: 'My book, O philosopher, is the nature of created things, and it is present when I want to read the words of God.' This essential atextuality of existence was at the heart of this religious lifestyle. It was recognized in the Celtic Church, too. The author of the tenth-century Welsh poem in the *Juvencus Manuscript*, in the University Library, Cambridge, tells us: 'The Father has made wonders in this world that it is difficult for us to find an equal number. Letters cannot contain it, letters cannot express it.' This equation of spirituality with nature is perhaps the most important element of Celtic religion that was played down and often ignored completely by Christians in later times.

In the fourth century, once Christianity had become the state religion of the empire, monasticism became fashionable, and people began to travel to the desert monasteries to see for themselves how the monks led the spiritual life. Travel books, describing the monastic life and the lives of the more famous monks, were popular and disseminated widely. As a response to this, outside the deserts, in western Europe, monasteries based on the desert model were founded. Among the most successful were at Marseilles and on the holy island of Lérins in southern Gaul, and Ligugé and Marmoutier, near Tours. Here, in imitation of the desert fathers, Christian monks attempted to separate themselves from the world, while, paradoxically, trying to convert Pagans, Stoics, Jews, Mithraists, Manichaeans, Zoroastrians, Atheists and Christians of other sects to their own beliefs.

At just the time when monastic ideas were fashionable, there was an important trade route that linked the western British Isles with the Mediterranean region. Archaeologists have discovered large amounts of pottery at post-Roman sites in southern Ireland, southwestern England and Wales, much of which originated in the eastern Mediterranean and

North Africa. Paradoxically, western Mediterranean artefacts are much less common. It was at this time that the Christian Fathers of the Egyptian desert became the main inspiration for Celtic monasticism, and links were forged between Egypt and the British Isles. Ireland, the major focus of Celtic Christianity, was not as remote as might first appear. In the sixth century, for instance, Cork was only three days' journey by sea from the Loire, and there was continuous maritime traffic. In the year 550, for example, 50 scholars from mainland Europe arrived in Ireland on one ship. They were visiting Ireland to study at the Celtic monastic schools, which had the reputation of being the best in western Europe.

During the period when the Celtic church was expanding and con- solidating its sphere of influence, the western Roman empire was in a state of dissolution. Enormous westward movements of populations from eastern and northeastern Europe brought slaves, refugees, emi- grants, pirates and invaders to most parts of western Europe. The southern and eastern parts of the old Roman province of Britain were taken over gradually by invaders and immigrants from what is now Holland, Denmark and north Germany. Areas which had become nominally Christian were re-Paganized either by the indigenous people reverting to their ancestral faith, or by the influx of Pagans from out- side. Many Britons fled westward for refuge in areas not yet conquered by the Germanic invaders. There was a revival of druidism in Gaul. Around the year 460, many Britons emigrated to Armorica, the north- western province of Gaul, which became the British colony called Little Britain, or Brittany. In the same period, northern Britain was being settled by Irish immigrants – the Scots. Irish invaders also settled in parts of what is now Wales and Cornwall. In this way, the north- western fringe of Europe gradually became identified as the homeland of the Celts. So it remains today, with the exception of Cumbria, where Celtic traditions are lost.

While Roman rule persisted in Britain, there was some missionary activity to the peripheral regions. In the year 397, St Ninian, a British priest, went northwards to preach Christianity to the Picts, and built a church in Galloway. The Christian religion entered Ireland seriously with the mission of St Patrick from 432 onwards. Patrick brought into Ireland a religion that had strong connections with the Coptic church of Egypt. While Britain was undergoing the turmoil of constant war- fare between indigenous Britons and invading Angles, Irishmen, Jutes, Picts and Saxons, the various tribes that lived in Ireland were spared the destruction. Thus Ireland more readily assimilated the Christian religion, which gradually absorbed and supplanted Paganism in both its religious and social functions. A new church grew up in Ireland, which, once established, began to spread beyond Ireland. The voyages of Irish monks are legendary, as recorded in the 'Life of St Brendan the Navigator' (*The Lives of the British Saints*, Honourable Society of Cymmrodorion, 1908) whose travels, though embellished and misinterpreted by later commentators, recount his voyages around the islands of the northwest Atlantic. Irish missionaries extended their sphere of influence into western Britain and then across the Channel into mainland Europe. In western Britain, where the Anglo-Saxons had not yet penetrated, British and Irish Celtic priests travelled around preaching, fighting and founding churches and monasteries. There, the great monastic settlements of Glastonbury and Malmesbury were founded by Irish monks. In Northumbria, East Anglia and Wessex, Anglian and Saxon churchmen were trained by Irish priests. Sometimes, English priests even crossed to Ireland, as in the case of Agilbercht, the mid-seventh-century Saxon Bishop of Wessex, who had received his training there.

Before the Scots invaded Britain from Ireland, the Picts inhabited the part of Britain north of the Clyde and Forth called Caledonia. Although the whole matter of the origin of the Picts is contentious, it is possible that ethnically they were a combination of indigenous Iron-Age peoples and later immigrant Celts. Around the year 501, Scots emigrated from Ulster to the Western Isles and Argyll, where they set up the kingdom of Dalriada as a colony dependent upon Ireland. A century later, under King Aidan, the Scots in Britain were secure enough to declare independence from the Scots who remained in Ireland. In the year 563, St Columba, who

In the year 563, St Columba … founded the monastery on the holy island of Iona. Through this base … Irish missionaries were able to extend their realm of operations into Scotland and then southwards into the Anglian kingdom of Northumbria.

was escaping from self-created trouble in Ireland, founded the monastery on the holy island of Iona. Through this base on Iona, Irish missionaries were able to extend their realm of operations into Scotland and then southwards into the Anglian kingdom of Northumbria. The monastery of Lindisfarne, which was the major Christian influence in Northumbria, was founded by Aidan of Iona in the year 635.

What is now southern Scotland was settled by Anglians from northern Germany, eventually being absorbed into the kingdom of Northumbria. The name of the city of Edinburgh – Edwinsborough, after the Northumbrian king Edwin – attests to the English presence here. Through this Anglian connection, Germanic elements were incorporated into Celtic art, leading to a Christian manuscript style that produced a perfect amalgamation of Celtic, Germanic and Coptic elements. During the last third of the seventh century, this art reached its most refined form. Although many fine manuscripts must have been lost over the years, and those which do survive may give a false impression, during the last third of the seventh century the full flowering of this style came into being in the *Book of Durrow*. In the next century, the *Lichfield Gospels*, the *Lindisfarne Gospels* and the *Book of Kells* appeared. During the eighth century, Celtic art continued to develop the symbolic, non-figurative patterns that reflect the aniconic traditions of Byzantine iconoclasm and the parallel Islamic prohibition on images. This style of work was disseminated through western Europe by the network of Celtic monasteries that stretched from Ireland to Austria and Italy. Artistic forms came into being then that were later used as key elements in the high medieval art of the so-called Gothic style.

During the eighth century, Celtic art continued to develop the symbolic, non-figurative patterns that reflect the aniconic traditions of Byzantine iconoclasm and the parallel Islamic prohibition on images.

In Anglian Northumbria, Celtic Christianity came into direct competition with Roman Catholicism. In the year 664, a church synod was held at Whitby to discuss the differences between Celtic and Catholic practice. Then, it was decided to abolish the usages of the Celtic church in England, and to replace them with Catholic practice. This assimilation of the Celtic church in England was the beginning of a process that finally eliminated the Celtic church completely. From Northumbria, Catholic influence moved northwards into the land of the Picts. The Pictish high king Nechtan IV mac Derile formally established Catholic Christianity in his kingdom in the year 710, and in 717 expelled the Celtic churchmen of Iona from his realms. After England went fully Catholic, Celtic Christianity continued in Scotland and Ireland. Gradually, Catholic practices took over from the Celtic, though in the eighth century the Culdees appeared as a reformed

Celtic movement. In Scotland, it was not until 1069 that Celtic Christian usages were abolished, when, at the insistence of his wife, King Malcolm Canmore declared Scotland fully Roman Catholic, like England.

THE CELTIC SPIRITUAL TRADITION

Although, geographically, the Celtic church in the British Isles may seem hopelessly isolated from Mediterranean religion, in actuality it was totally cosmopolitan. Celtic Christianity was composed of many threads: it took the practices and theories from Egyptian, Greek and Frankish Christians while retaining and adapting elements of Celtic and Classical Paganism. According to the nineteenth-century Welsh bard, the Reverend J. Williams ab Ithel: 'The Bards believed that all things were tending to perfection; when, therefore, they embraced Christianity, they must on their own principles have viewed it as a stage in advance of their former creed.' Thus, there was continuity and not a break between Paganism and Christianity. Celtic Christianity allowed its priests to travel widely. Many did not spend their lives cooped up in caves or monastic cells; rather they made regular journeys across mainland Europe, through the old Celtic heartlands to the Mediterranean. Celtic priests were the founders of many of the greatest monasteries of Europe, through which learning was maintained and disseminated.

In the bardic tradition of the Pagan Celts, where knowledge and understanding were the most prized abilities in a person, the Celtic priests were naturally highly learned men. While the Roman Empire in the West was breaking up, the monastic schools in Ireland were recognized as the best in western Europe. As Gregory of Tours lamented in the sixth century: 'Culture and education are perishing, dying out in every city of Gaul .... People often complain "Alas for our times, literacy is dying among us, and no man can be found among our people who can write down the events of the present day".' However, that was not the case in Ireland. Bede tells us how: 'In Ireland, there were many Englishmen, both noble and low-born, who travelled from their homeland in the time of Bishops Finan and Colman ... some soon bound themselves by a monastic vow, but others thought it better to travel around the cells of various teachers for the joy of reading. The Irish welcomed them all, provided them with food and lodging free of charge, lent them their books and taught them without a fee.'

In a real way, the Celtic monks were the inheritors of the Celto-Roman tradition, continuing and preserving classical and druidic learning as well as teaching Christianity. For example, the Irish priest Columbanus, known as 'Prince of Druids', who founded several monasteries in mainland Europe, was one of the most learned men of his age. In addition to his priestly role, Columbanus was a noted poet who wrote in Greek according to classical modes. Many of the founders of the Celtic church came from the upper class, which in Pagan times had provided the druids and temple priests. The genealogies of the British Saints who founded Christianity in Britain after the fall of Rome show them all to be members of one or other of the Eight Noble Families of Britain.

Thus, the leaders of the new religion took the same career path as their Pagan forebears, and in Ireland we can see that many Celtic Christian priests took over almost imperceptibly from the druids. They continued all of the druidic functions, reinterpreting their more Pagan elements according to Christian beliefs and practices. So, for example, when St Patrick, St Carantoc and other members of the High King's legal commission reformed the laws of Ireland, they brought in Christian elements, but left as much of the traditional structure in place as possible. Just as the role of the druid as law-giver was taken over by the church, so other social functions were transferred from the Pagan to the Christian priesthood. Thus, St Findchua took over the role of official curser for the King of Leinster when the druid who should have performed the traditional battle-rite was found to be too old to conduct it. So the Christian priest substituted for the druid, and kept the job, later handing it on to his successors.

The leaders of the new religion took the same career path as their Pagan forebears, and in Ireland ... many Celtic Christian priests took over almost imperceptibly from the druids.

If the priestly caste remained little altered when Christianity arrived, then neither were the ancestral sacred places of the Celts tampered with greatly. Holy places in the Celtic landscape are the collective shrines of the community, maintained by the families which legally own them. Because in traditional society land could not be bought and sold, but only inherited, Celtic holy places were the hereditary property of families. Any man who became a priest in the Celtic church maintained his hereditary rights over the ancestral holy places in his family's ownership. In Pagan times, priesthood was hereditary, and the Celtic church did not alter the custom. Thus, holy places owned by a druid family would become Christian when the leading member of the family became a Christian monk or priest. Many of the ancient monasteries in Celtic lands are on such land.

Gradually, as time passed, the ancestral holy places of the Celts were altered by Christian worship, during which process the older practices were not obliterated but absorbed. In the Celtic realms, vernacular customs and usages of Pagan origin were observed alongside the official liturgy of the church. Local traditions and myths of the old gods, goddesses and heroes were re-stated as episodes in the lives of saints. Thus, traditional society was not disrupted by the new religion, but retained its continuity and stability. The main difference was that the patriarchal nature of the Christian church now excluded women from most of their traditional religious roles, such as being seeresses and guardians of women's shrines. Sometimes women were expelled from their traditional places, as in the shameful incident when St Columba expelled all cows and women from the holy isle of Iona, on the pretext that: 'Where there is a cow, there is a woman, and where there is a woman, there is mischief.'

> *Gradually, as time passed, the ancestral holy places of the Celts were altered by Christian worship, during which process the older practices were not obliterated but absorbed.*

THE STRUCTURE OF CELTIC CHRISTIANITY

The Celtic church had four grades of brethren, reflecting the quaternary structure of the land of Ireland, the symbolic image of wholeness. At the lowest level were the *Juniores Alumni*, students who served; above them, the *Operarii*, lay brothers, who did the manual labour; above them, the *Seniores*, elders, dedicated to prayer and teaching; and over the whole community ruled the head, *Abba Pater* or *Pater Spiritualis*, who lived apart from the others on higher ground. The four circles inherent in the Celtic Cross reflect this four-fold organization so prevalent in Celtic culture. Apart from their autonomy from the church of the four Patriarchs, one of the objections made by the orthodox against the Celtic church was that their tonsure was non-Christian. The druids had tonsured themselves in styles according to which order they belonged, and the Celtic monastic tonsure was condemned as a version of this, or that worn by the theurgic sage Simon Magus and his followers. However, whatever its origin, it was clearly non-Catholic, and the tonsure was altered immediately the Celtic church was absorbed into the Roman sphere of influence after the Synod of Whitby. The *Annals* of Mac Firbis tell us that then: 'The tonsure of St Peter the Apostle was taken by the family of Iona, for it was the tonsure of Simon Magus they had until then, as had Colum Cille (Columba) himself.'

At first, Celtic monasteries were no more than small aggregations of cells, caves or huts, where a few monks lived together but remained relatively independent of one another. Soon they grew, however, and expanded to create new, centralized settlements. In Britain, Irish monks founded the monasteries at Iona, Lindisfarne, Glastonbury, Malmesbury and Burgh Castle near Great Yarmouth. Also, by the seventh century, Celtic monastic settlements had been made in mainland Europe. Then, the largest Celtic monastery of all was at Bangor on Belfast Lough. Reputed to have 3,000 monks, Bangor was the focus for missionary activities all over western Europe. From there, St Sinell, tutor of St Columbanus, travelled south in 589 and founded the monastery of Bobbio, near Milan in Italy.

In turn, Columbanus founded the monastery of Luxeuil, in the Celtic sacred land of the Vosges. Later, he moved on to Fontaines, and then Bobbio in the Italian Apennines. He and his followers are said to have founded around 100 monasteries. One of the most attractive locations was an earthly reflection of the otherworldly Celtic Avalon, the holy island of Reichenau in Lake Constance, which became a fertile monastic settlement. Elsewhere, Celtic monks founded the monasteries of St Gall, St Bertin, Jumièges, St Riquier, Remirement, Jouarre, Chelles, Noirmoutier, Echternach, Hanau, Lagny and Würzburg. These monasteries and others served as a network of hostels for Celtic pilgrims on their way to Rome, Egypt and Jerusalem. As well as travelling overland, Irish priests were remarkable seamen. From Ireland, Celtic monks first settled Iona, then founded further monasteries in the Orkneys and Shetland Islands, where the islands named 'Papa' attest to their widespread travels. They reached the Faeroes shortly after the year 700. They and their descendants lived there until around 860, when they were dispossessed by the Norse. Finally, Irish churchmen discovered Iceland in the 790s, but they made no permanent settlements there until Celtic Christians went with the first Norse settlers.

Nevertheless, despite its pioneering activities in the former Celtic heartland, the Celtic church was the loser in a power struggle with the centralized church of Rome. Better-organized Benedictine monasticism was on the increase. Gradually, the Benedictine rule ousted the stricter Columbanian rule of the Celtic monasteries. By now isolated from its eastern Mediterranean roots, the strength of the Celtic church proved to be unequal to the power of the Roman church, and at the Synod of Whitby in 664 the Celts were ordered to adopt Roman usages, effectively amalgamating the Celtic with the Roman church. Finally, the Synod of Autun in 670 made the Benedictine rule compulsory in monasteries in France, supplanting the Celtic rule. Benedict's rule was much less harsh and exacting than the strict asceticism that by then had become the norm in Celtic Christianity, and hence it was a more attractive proposition for the aspiring monk. However, there *was* a place for the Celtic Cross in the new Romanized system.

The strength of the Celtic church proved to be unequal to the power of the Roman church, and at the Synod of Whitby in 664 the Celts were ordered to adopt Roman usages.

2
PRECEDENTS AND ORIGINS

In many ways, the Celtic Cross is a continuation and refinement of a number of aspects of traditional spiritual culture. Most fundamentally, it contains symbolic elements that express the relationship of human beings to the divine. These elements are transcendent of religious doctrine, belonging to the perennial philosophy which underlies all religions.

THE NAVEL OF THE WORLD

The concept of the navel of the world, now called by its Greek name, *omphalos*, was recognized as far back as ancient Egyptian times. The Egyptian world centre was more than a symbolic or theoretical place, for it was actually represented by an elliptical stone that marked the mid-point of the country. This was the geodetic point of reference at the place where the north–south meridian and the east–west parallel crossed each other. In the Old Kingdom, the centre of Egypt was at Sakkara. The *omphalos* there was marked by the holy stone of Sokar, god of orientation. Drawings of it in ancient papyri show that it was flanked by images of two birds of prey, alluding to a legend known later from Greece. In the twelfth dynasty, the geodetic centre of Egypt was changed, and the Sakkara *omphalos* was replaced by another stone in the Temple of Amun at Thebes. This may have been the inspiration for a later and more famous *omphalos* at Delphi in Greece. The Delphic *omphalos* was the seat of the priestess known as the Pythia. She was the oracle of Apollo, the god who, in the words of Plato, 'sits in the centre of the navel of the earth'. According to legend, Delphi was discovered by Zeus, who, as grand geometer of the cosmos, measured the earth. From the Olympian heights, he sent forth two eagles to find the middle of the world. Zeus released one bird to the east, and the other to the west. Flying in straight lines, they met each other over Delphi, which was defined thus as the navel of the world. According to another legend, this was also the place where Apollo slew with his arrow the serpent called Python so that the oracular goddess could take her place there without hindrance.

At least from Mycenean times, around 1400 BCE, if not earlier, the Delphic world navel was marked by a *baitylos*, an unworked mark-stone which was regarded as an aniconic emblem of the deity. Later, this rough stone was considered inappropriate and was replaced by a finely carved *omphalos*. This was also an elliptical stone to which an eagle of gold was attached on each side in the Egyptian manner. This Delphic omphalos was carved with swags of what appear to be wool or cloth, recreating the patterns made upon the earlier stone when it was honoured ceremonially. A number of ancient Greek sculptured reliefs and vase-paintings show the *omphalos* in the days when it was the revered sacred object of the oracle, dressed with ribbons and branches. The Roman writer Varro compared its shape with that of a 'treasury', and when Delphi was sacked by the Celts under Brennos in 279 BCE the actual treasure of Apollo's shrine was taken away as booty.

Representation of an *omphalos*-stone on an altar, *c.* 400 BCE, from an ancient Greek vase in Berlin.

Although it is primarily the navel of the world, there is a strong connection, not only linguistically, between the *omphalos* and the phallus. A number of *omphaloi* at other places were phallic in shape, and the Etruscans used phalloid stones as tomb-markers. In the Celtic realms, a comparable pillar-stone stood at Pfalzfeld in the Hunsrück, Germany, in the land once inhabited by the Treviri tribe. Surrounded by ropework, an Etruscan motif that later appears in Celtic crosses all over the British Isles, the carvings on this stone include a bearded human head with horns or a head-dress, surrounded by scrollwork in La Tène style. In Ireland, similar stone *omphaloi* have survived. The stone at Turoe in County Galway is an elliptical mark-stone that closely resembles the Delphic *omphalos* in shape and size, even down to the swirling patterns that spiral across its surface. Elsewhere in Ireland are stones that include a cushion-shaped *omphalos* at Castlestrange in County Roscommon and a stone at Mullaghmast in Kildare. The latter is the base of an ancient Pagan pillar. Another base of a round pillar, which, when intact, was probably approximately conical, exists at Killycluggan in County Cavan. These *omphalos*-pillars are the model from which the later designers of the Irish high crosses took their inspiration.

The concept of the stone that stands at the centre of the world, or, by association, the centre of a country or sacred area, was known else-where in northern Europe. Before the introduction of the Christian religion into western Norway, many sacred places possessed *Hellige hvide stene* (holy white stones). Many have been discovered beneath churches or old homesteads which in Pagan times served as places of worship. The *Hellige hvide stene* are cylindrical pillars terminating with a hemisphere, made from white stone, either marble, quartzite or gran-ite. Phallic in form, and measuring up to 90 cm (3 ft) in height, it is likely that these stones were the objects of worship of the god of sexu-ality and generation, Yngvi-Frey, who was the chief god of the older, pre-agricultural Norse pantheon, known as the Vanir. When the Christian religion was introduced, the holy white stones were buried, to be re-discovered in modern times. In Scotland, Clackmannan, a for-mer inauguration-place of the Pictish kings, possesses a similar, but much larger, phallic megalith which stands by the church. Like other *omphaloi*, it hallows the centre-point of the land, where the spiritual essence is at its height. Such places were the natural spiritual centres of the priesthood, monarchs and lords. In England, the London Stone, recently refurbished, traditionally marks the centre and holds the 'luck' of the city of London, while the same function is ascribed to the Blue Stane of St Andrews in Scotland. In the Low Countries, the central points of town market-places, which in other places would be marked by a market cross, were marked by a blue stone. Thus, the tradition of the *omphalos* lives on as an integral element of modern cities.

NATURAL PHENOMENA

Another forerunner of the Celtic Cross can be seen in a striking natur-al phenomenon. Under certain weather conditions, sun- or moonlight shining through airborne ice crystals produces halo phenomena. These are more common in northern latitudes, and there are many

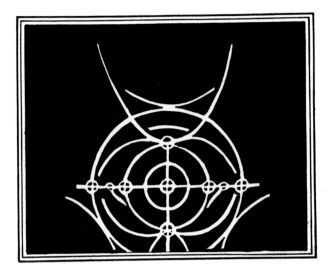

The patterns of sun-dogs, rings and crosses that surround the sun under certain icy conditions in northern latitudes. As manifestations of the cosmic realms, they appear to be the origin of the sunwheel as a holy symbol.

RIGHT: An early sunwheel-cross at St Dogmael's Abbey, Dyfed, west Wales. *(Nigel Pennick)*

recorded patterns of solar and lunar haloes, including arcs, circles and crosses, which have been exhaustively investigated by contemporary meteorologists. However, when one actually sees these events, they are most impressive, and no amount of scientific explanation can diminish their awesome effect upon the observer. Thus, in ancient times, they were seen as direct manifestations of the power of the solar and lunar deities. Most common among the many possible patterns is the sun-dog array, in which a parhelic spot of light or 'mock sun' appears on either side of the real sun, 22 degrees away from the sun's disc. Sometimes, from the 'mock suns' develops a circle that can produce a full sunwheel or even more complex patterns. The most important halo form in the present context is the sunwheel, which is a cross surrounded by a circle, with the actual sun at the centre and 'mock suns' at the four quarters. Also, according to many eye-witnesses over the years, spirit-lights that emanate from the earth sometimes take the form of an *omphalos*, a pillar, a *tau* or even a wheel-cross. St Trillo's seaside holy well chapel at Llandrillo-yn-Rhôs (Rhos-on-Sea) in north Wales was founded at a place where the saint saw a Celtic Cross of light emerge from the ground.

Quartered circles like this are common in Cretan artefacts from the Minoan period, and they are also known widely in Northern Europe in carvings dating from the Bronze Age. There are numerous examples of the quartered circle in Scandinavian rock-carvings, which may date from as early as 1500 BCE, and certainly no later than 500 BCE. These wheels are considered by almost all observers to be the solar symbol, the sunwheel, and it is likely that wherever they occur they are all intended to represent this remarkable phenomenon. Among the many carvings,

there are several variant forms of the wheel. The pattern that was adopted later by the Celtic Christian church, and taken to be the basic form, is the four-spoked wheel. Although it is by far the most common, however, it is not the only form, as the number of spokes are variable. There are also examples composed of two concentric circles. In the Scandinavian rock-carvings, these forms appear in the same contexts, and thus are assumed to be versions of one another rather than completely different symbols. The circles may be shown alone, or with appendages that can be interpreted as supports. Sometimes they are carried by human figures, either above the head or as shields. They are borne on ships, and depicted as the wheels of actual vehicles.

Bronze Age rock-carvings of sunwheels from Sweden and Norway.
(1–4) Bohuslän;
(5) Östfold;
(6–7) Bohuslän;
(8) Östergötland;
(9) S.W. Norway;
(10) Bohuslän;
(11–12) Östergötland.

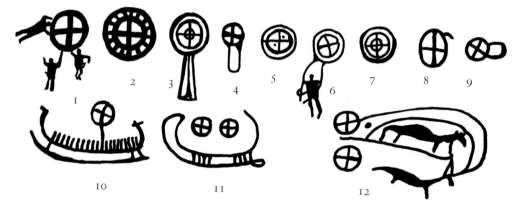

Some of the rock-carvings from Bohuslän in Sweden show figures that might be interpreted as the wheel symbol set up on some kind of support, such as a wooden or wickerwork framework. If this is the case, then the Celtic Cross has a direct precedent in the ceremonial symbolism of ancient northern-European solar Paganism. Two of the stone slabs that once lined the Bronze-Age burial cist inside the mound called Bredarör at Kivik in Scania, southern Sweden, have the fourfold wheel, perfectly delineated. They have been dated as *c.* twelfth century BCE. Similar wheel-carvings exist elsewhere in ancient Europe. For example, at Carpene di Sellero in the southern alpine valley of Valcamonica, there are many such sunwheels dated at around 500 BCE.

THE WHEEL SYMBOL

As the means by which a vehicle travels, the wheel was a sacred object in its own right. In Pagan times, vehicles were buried frequently with their Celtic owners, perhaps to serve as the conveyance of the dead person in the otherworld. Both the sun and moon, worshipped as deities, were portrayed as driving chariots through the sky. In northern Europe, ritual vehicles were used to transport images of deities around the country in sacred journeys that sanctified or cleansed the land. Wagons accompanied the dead in La Tène period tumuli, the wheels being detached and ranged along the walls of the burial chamber. Even in Christian times, images of Jesus mounted on a wheeled donkey were pushed through the streets on Palm Sunday, perhaps in continuation of the rites of the wheel-god.

By themselves, wheels appear in Celtic Paganism as an attribute of the heavenly thunder-and-lightning god, Taranis, 'The Thunderer', whom the Romans assimilated with Jupiter, and the British Christians with God the Father under the title Daronwy. The wheel-god Taranis was acknowledged by the Pagan Celts from the Balkans to the British Isles. Remains of the worship of the wheel-god have been found all over the Celtic realms. They range from coins, small wheel-brooches and votive images to lifesize statues of the deity. The shrine site at Cold Kitchen Hill in Wiltshire has yielded many wheel-form brooches and votive wheels, which can be seen in Devizes Museum. Sometimes, deities are portrayed with wheels. One is carved on the left side of a Roman altar dedicated to the Great God Jupiter, kept at Tullie House, Carlisle. A Gallo-Roman altar of Jupiter found at Laudun in Gard, France, shows the god holding a sceptre in his left hand, while on the right is an eagle and a five-spoked wheel. Another statue of Jupiter, found at Vaison in Vaucluse, France, shows the standing god holding a wheel, accompanied by an eagle.

Elsewhere, the wheel-god is depicted on the first-century BCE Celto-Thracian silver cauldron from Gundestrup in Denmark, while in medieval East Anglia the wheel-god became the hero-giant Tom Hickathrift, who saved the people of the Cambridgeshire Fens by defeating the fearsome giant of Wisbech. Hickathrift's weapons were not a sword and shield. Instead, he used the axle-tree of a cart as a quarter-

Wheels appear in Celtic Paganism as an attribute of the heavenly thunder-and-lightning god, Taranis, 'The Thunderer'.

staff, and a wheel as a shield. Hickathrift and the giant are shown on a seventeenth-century pargeted wall of the old Sun Inn at Saffron Walden in Essex. In Huntingdonshire, a similar figure, called Old Hub, appeared alongside the molly dancers at the midsummer festivities, marking the high point of the sun in the year.

The wheel is the most significant attribute of the Celtic Cross, and it appeared in a pre-Christian context along with the columnar form on Roman columns dedicated to Jupiter. A different representation of the wheel-column can be seen on a pagan Roman grave-stela in Carlisle Museum. In the form of a rectangular slab surmounted by a triangular pediment containing a lunar crescent, it bears three wheel-crosses. One is at the apex of the pediment, while the other two are at the junction of the rectangle and the triangle. They are depicted as supported on bulbous pillars in the manner of Celtic Crosses. From this, it is possible that pillars with wheel-crosses existed in Roman times as Pagan, rather than Christian, monuments. In support of this hypothesis, there are Christian Anglo-Saxon representations of crosses which closely resemble their pre-Christian forerunners. The Lechmere stone at Hanley Castle, Hereford and Worcester, is a fine example of this type of cross.

In later iconography, the sunwheel was taken from the Pagan sun gods and goddesses and used as a symbol of the Christian godhead. The *Fuldauer Sakramentar* in the University Library at Göttingen, dating from around the year 975, shows this in a remarkable image of traditional cosmology. One illuminated page is in the form of a diagram composed of three circles. The outermost circle contains personifications of the seasons and months. Inside this, the second circle has the four elements, while the central circle is reserved for God. In his hands, he holds the heads of the sun and the moon, while beside him on either side are two golden six-spoked wheels. In Classical art, the sun-god Helios is depicted riding in the car of the sun, a wheeled vehicle pulled by four horses. This image was perpetuated in the Eastern Orthodox church in the shape of Profitis Elias, the Jewish prophet Elijah, who flew to heaven.

The wheel is the most significant attribute of the Celtic Cross, and it appeared in a pre-Christian context along with the columnar form on Roman columns dedicated to Jupiter.

Orthodox icons still being made today at the monastery of Mount Athos depict the prophet, whose Greek name Elias is a continuation of Helios, riding heavenwards in a chariot of fire pulled by the four horses of the sun. Sometimes the chariot of Profitis Elias is shown inside a roundel at the centre of a cross, in place of Christ. As a holy sign, the wheel was employed by Romanesque sculptors. In southern Germany, a carving of the wheel god is prominent on the monastery tower at Hirsau in the Black

Forest, and it is the central feature of the tympanum of the main entrance of the cathedral of Jaca in Spain.

As a more abstract symbol, the sunwheel has continued to be a protective sigil until the present day. It was stamped by the Germanic Pagans on the funeral urns in which they buried the ashes of their dead. Also, as the *Circle of Columbkille*, the sunwheel cross was the talismanic sigil of St Columba. Celtic Christians used it to invoke his power as a protection against all harm. Sacred signs inscribed within a circle have a long history as magical talismans. Known generally as insigils, they play an important role in protection. Medieval Irish magicians ascribed great magical power to the circular design called Feisefin, the Wheel of Fionn MacCumhaill (the Irish hero Finn McCool). Consisting of a circle on which certain letters are written in the ogham alphabet, Fionn's wheel was used as a protective talisman against harm from other human beings, or evil spirits. The Northern Tradition magic of Scandinavia and Britain uses similar insigils with bind-runes.

THE TORC

The most characteristic artefact of Celtic culture is another round structure, the torc, which is literally a binding of metal. Originating in the fifth century BCE during the La Tène period, the torc is essentially a body ornament made of precious metal in the form of a curved rod with identical free ends that face one another, almost touching. In effect, torcs are incomplete circles. Worn on the neck or arm, they must be flexible enough to enable the wearer to put them on and take them off, but without damaging or breaking the metal. Torcs appear to have had a sacred meaning, for images of the gods show them wearing torcs around their necks, or holding them in their hands. Among the wealth of magnificent ancient Celtic artefacts, some of the most masterly craftsmanship is preserved in the torcs. One of the most remarkable collection of torcs comes from the splendid hoard found at Snettisham in Norfolk, England. Dating from the first century BCE, the treasure consists of golden torcs composed of exquisite ropework in metal. One of the more notable examples is in the form of a rope composed of eight strands, each strand of which is made of eight twisted golden rods. The fineness of detail and the regularity of the twined metal in these torcs is a demonstration of the highest skills possessed by the ancient Celtic goldsmiths. These wonderful ancient Celtic torcs are displayed in the British Museum.

While the curved bodies of torcs were composed of ornamented rods or ropework of precious metal, their terminals were fashioned into geometric forms or animal heads. A heavy silver torc from Trichtingen in southern Germany is a fine example. The Trichtingen torc has opposing terminals in the shape of bulls' heads, each of which wears a torc around his neck. There are literary references to Celtic torc terminals in the shape of dogs and other animals, as well as knob- and ring-shaped endings. The twisted ropework of the torc is an early example of the Celtic motif of the entwined or interlaced rope, which appears later in various ornamental and symbolic forms on Celtic Crosses. Like torcs, Iron Age Celtic chains are remarkable examples of the smith's craft where hard metal has been transformed into a flexible structure whose patterns prefigure the ornament on later Celtic Crosses. The smiths who made them went far beyond mere utilitarian design, creating remarkable interweavings of skilfully patterned iron links. A related Celtic invention in the military field was chainmail, introduced around 300 BCE, and soon adopted by the Romans and other military powers. Like the torcs, chainmail shows the Celtic love of interpenetration of materials, in which individual rings of the hardest iron are interlocked to create an impenetrable, yet flexible, armour.

ROMAN MOSAICS

The patterns of Roman mosaics are important forerunners of the designs used to adorn and embellish the much later Celtic Crosses. Basic crosses are present as patterns in the tesselation designs of early Roman mosaics in Britain. For example, a mosaic from the Roman palace at Fishbourne in Sussex, made between the years 70 and 100, is patterned with equal-armed crosses. Another monochrome labyrinth mosaic dating from the fourth century, found at Cirencester, is concentric around an equal-armed cross at the centre. Roman labyrinth mosaics in general are constructed in a cross-form. Most are square, but there are a number of round forms known. A polychrome mosaic found in London in 1805 during the construction of the Bank of England, illustrated here, has an equal-armed cross set within a circle that itself is surrounded by a square panel of interlace. The circles or scrolls at the ends of the cross-arms are similar to the treatment of many later representations of crosses and Trees of Life on runestones.

Many Roman mosaics contain panels surrounded by the interlace pattern known as the guilloche chain. The fact that mosaic researchers

A cross from a panel of a Roman mosaic discovered in 1805 on the future site of the Bank of England, London, preserved in the British Museum.

use this specialized name for the interlace has tended to distance the pattern from its later derivatives. There are two basic forms of guilloche chain. One is a simple twist of two separate 'ribbons', while the other is usually composed of three 'ribbons' interlaced in the manner of much Celtic work. This form, which appears later throughout Celtic, Nordic and Romanesque art, was used universally in Roman mosaic. It was clearly an influence upon this kind of Celtic interlace pattern.

The wheel-cross actually appears in Roman mosaic work, as it does on tomb stelae. One fine example is in the mosaic of Orpheus found at Littlecote Park in Wiltshire. Dating from around the year 360, it has a wheel-cross roundel with an image of lyre-playing Orpheus at the centre. In the four quarters made by the cross are four goddesses, riding various beasts sidesaddle. They symbolize the four directions, the four elements and the four seasons. Later Christian cross-makers sometimes re-used this perennial motif by presenting Christ at the same place as the centre of the four elements within the circle.

3

ARCHAIC CELTIC STONES

In the Hallstatt period, generally after 1000 BCE, the Celts lived in central Europe, for they had not yet migrated westwards and northwards to the British Isles. However, Celtic traditions there are recognizable as forerunners of what came later. In that period, the Celts set up aniconic stones as holy stopping-places in the landscape. In their form and location, they pre-figure the later Celtic Crosses. Many have a roughly humanoid form that continues the much older tradition of making stone representations of the female principle. Some of the central European stones, such as the Hallstatt period pillar-cross from Tübingen-Kilchberg in south Germany (now in the Württembergisches Landesmuseum in Stuttgart), have a 'head' part that is incised with an X-shape. Dating from 1,000 years or more before the Christians adopted the cross, these stones resemble the much later Celtic stone crosses in parts of Cornwall and Wales. Even when the Celtic Cross had become a stylized form, certain sculptors made cross-es that echo the shouldered humanoid forms of the earlier Continental stones. Surviving examples of this kind of 'goddess-cross' can be seen in west Wales at Carew and Nevern. A true goddess-stone like those on which the crosses are based still stands in its original position just outside the churchyard of St Martin's in Guernsey. She is La Gran'mère du Chimiquère, a Celtic goddess image which was revered there long before the church was built. In the form of a female Herm, 'The Grandmother of the Cemetery' is an armless stone figure with breasts and a radiate collar that resembles the patterns on some Celtic images in Germany.

A pointed stone with a rudimentary human face from Rottenburg, at Stammheim in Stuttgart, is an early type of humanoid stone. It is a megalith whose shape roughly suggested the human form, which was 'humanized' by having the suggestion of a face carved onto it. Later, actual human representations were carved by the Celts. Some appear to

RIGHT: Pre-Celtic carved stones from central Europe. *Left:* carved menhir from Algund, South Tyrol, Italy, with axes, swords and wagon. *Right:* stele from Weilheim, near Tübingen, Germany, *c.* 2000 BCE, sculpted with weapons.

BELOW: The Husjatyn god-pillar from the River Zbrucz in Galicia, Poland, with images of the deities of the Pagan Slavs, is a direct parallel of the Celtic pillar-stones and the Roman Jupiter Columns.

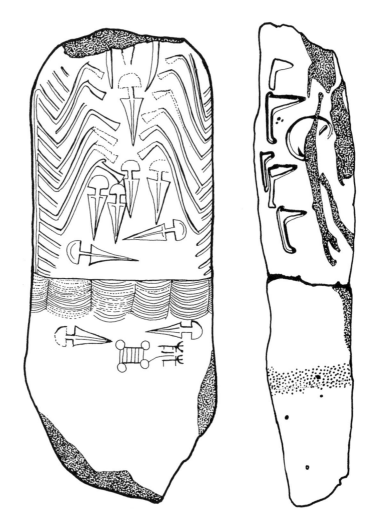

have been images of goddesses and gods, while others served as commemorative memorials to individuals. It is thought that the Celts took the idea of setting up memorial images of the deceased individual from the Etruscans. There was a similar tradition among the Pagan Slavs further east. They erected carved stone pillars in honour of deities such as Triglav, Svantovit and Gerovit. They were often square-section pillars with faces of the gods carved at the top. The Polish Husjatyn pillar, illustrated here, is a typical example. Its cap resembles the capstones on the Irish high crosses at Ahenny.

In addition to ancestral memorials, there were also representations of deities in animal form, for in European Paganism animals can be manifestations of the divine equally as well as the human form. Thus, in addition to goddesses and gods, the boar, deer, stag, horse, dog and wolf appear frequently in sacred art. Although animal attributes accompany many Celtic carvings of humanoid deities, they also appear by themselves on Gallic and Pictish memorials and in certain contexts on later Celtic Crosses. In addition to the spirits of the animal world, Celtic cosmology recognizes intermediate beings that exist somewhere between the human and the animal. They appear as human-animal form images that include serpent-footed and horned men.

Horns and the horn-like 'leaf-crown' surmount the human head in many La Tène carvings. These seem to pre-figure both the form of the wheel-head of crosses and the haloes surrounding the heads of saints and the deity in Christian iconography. This halo-like form appears in the hairstyles of Celtic goddesses such as Epona and The Mothers. Two-faced figures also appear in Pagan Celtic art. Usually called janiform, after the Roman god Janus, they seem to have originated in Etruscan practice. The most striking of these La Tène janiform images is a larger-than-life size, two-faced stone figure that was discovered at Holzgerlingen in Baden-Württemberg, Germany. This was a pillar in the form of a sculpted humanoid, with the figure's arms held tightly across the waist; the two-faced head had a pair of horns that took the form of a separated 'leaf crown'. Other multiple representations include the sculpture of a three-faced male deity from Soissons

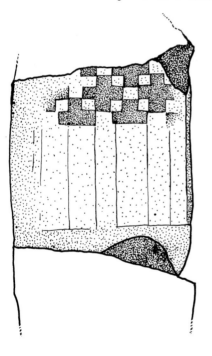

in France. This is so skilfully designed that there is a central face whose left and right eyes become respectively the right and left eyes of the other faces. All three have ears of wheat for beards, while the carving below of a cock and a ram infer a connection with the Roman god Mercury.

The lower part of another Celtic image from Steinenbronn, also kept in Stuttgart, shows how the human figure melds into the stone cross. Dating from the fourth century BCE, this stone bears patterns that demonstrate the multivalency of Celtic

LEFT: The lower part of a broken Celtic stone figure found at Steinenbronn, Baden-Württemberg, Germany, c. 400 BCE, carved with T- and cross-tesselation patterns that appear later in Christian Celtic art.

A horned Celtic pillar-image of the fifth century BCE. Reconstruction at a tumulus in the Federlesmahd woodland at Leinfelden-Echterdingen, Baden-Württemberg, Germany. *(Nigel Pennick)*

design. Perhaps representing a costume, the patterns fade from a tesse-lation of Ts and crosses into a rectangular grid which in turn gives way to swirling patterns that may represent the phases of the moon. The tesselated pattern, which contained crosses 400 years before the Christian religion came into being, appears in Britain much later in Celtic manuscripts and on crosses, showing the continuity of Celtic art over time and distance. Humanoid Celtic pillar-stones have also been discovered in the British Isles. The so-called serpent stone from Maryport, Cumbria, is a carved stone phallus with a human head at the top. A humanoid pillar-stone at Minnigaff in Dumfries and Galloway has a bearded human head at the top on one side, whle bearing a cross with a bird on the other. The head tops a pillar which has no other carving. Thus it resembles the *Herms* and *Xoana* that were characteristic monuments of European Paganism.

PAGAN AND CHRISTIAN IMAGES

In the early Christian period, the distinction between what constituted a Pagan and a Christian image was unclear. In every age, Celtic artists have juxtaposed suitable elements from different sources. They have never adopted images haphazardly, but always in an appropriate way that reinforced whatever archetype of primordial holiness was required by the spiritual scheme they sought to portray. Thus, on Celtic Crosses, we find representations that can be interpreted equally as representing different myths. So there is the image that can be interpreted as the archetype of the hunter, Daniel amid the lions, or the hero or god, such as Odin, who overcomes or else is devoured by the beasts. Many Celtic images that were made after Christianity was introduced show no discrimination between Pagan and Christian images. Rather, Pagan and Christian elements are juxtaposed in such a way that emphasizes their similarities rather than their differences. So, instead of bringing division, they reinforce the archetype of holiness that is represented by a specific character from the Christian canon. Thus, traditional Celtic sacred elements which originated in the Pagan La Tène era appear alongside images of Christian priests and themes from Christian mythology. They are a continual reminder that in the Celtic lands there was no break, but a gradual, seamless transition between Pagan and Christian culture.

However, images depicting specifically Christian subjects in Celtic art are different from Pagan ones. This is not because of any noticeable difference in artistic or stylistic treatment, but because without exception they illustrate episodes and themes from written Biblical texts. Although they also follow iconographical conventions, Pagan images illustrate an oral narrative of sacred stories. In general, Pagan images represent the pictorial language of myth, while Christian ones come from a literate structure. Thus, the Pagan images are nearer to folk art than are the Christian ones. While the church sought to edit the scriptures to produce a definitive text of the Christian stories and doctrines, in the Pagan, oral culture, there was no rigid narrative. Because the druids committed nothing to writing and relied on memory, there was no orthodoxy in the sense of 'religions of the book'. Oral myth lives in action, word and image, not in books. This is why it is often rather difficult to identify images of Pagan goddesses and gods, whose artistic attributes may be based upon oral traditions that are lost now, such as the episodes from the life of Loki on several Manx crosses.

Because the druids committed nothing to writing and relied on memory, there was no orthodoxy in the sense of 'religions of the book'.

A number of ancient Celtic churches contain some quite remarkable images within their fabric or churchyards. Close to the high cross at Cardonagh in Donegal is a stone pillar with an image of a priest with a bell. His form is similar to earlier Pagan images that exist *in situ* in Brittany, such as the twin images at Elven, Morbihan, called Jean and Jeanne Babouin. Standing in a line inside the unroofed twelfth-century church on Boa Island in Lower Lough Erne, County Fermanagh, is a splendid colection of seven stone humanoid figures that date from around the year 900. They are both Pagan and Christian, including a *sheela-na-gig*, a seated man holding a book, an abbot or abbess with crozier and bell, and a squat figure in the cross-legged Celtic sitting position often associated with the antlered god Cernunnos. This figure has a large, horned, two-faced head. He appears again on a humanoid pillar-stone at Cardonagh, County Donegal, while a similar, squatting, antlered figure is present on the north cross at Clonmacnois.

At Rougham in County Clare stands another pillar-stone. This is in the form of a *tau* cross, the symbol of St Anthony of Egypt favoured by medieval stonemasons. It is carved with Celtic heads on the upper side. The churchyard of Caldragh has a two-faced janiform stone image which has a depression, perhaps for libations, between the heads. A curious stone preserved in the Margam Stones Museum in south Wales depicts an ithyphallic man. In his hands he holds two small phallus-shaped staves. Although the actual names and sometimes the meanings of these figures are forgotten in many places, the old Pagan deities are still remembered occasionally. One such instance is at Kirk Conchan, near Douglas on the Isle of Man, where there is a dog-headed image depicting the Manx Celtic god, Conchem, who has been assimilated with the Christian saint, Christopher. A number of stone crosses with dog carvings are known from this place.

The Celts were known for their cult of the human head, in which they decapitated their enemies and preserved their heads as sacred objects. The Celto-Ligurian shrines at Roqueperteuse and Entremont in Bouches-du-Rhône in the south of France are among the best documented of the Celtic head shrines. Because these sacred structures were destroyed in antiquity by the Romans, the cult skulls were pre-served in the ruins. There, archaeologists discovered human heads placed in niches of the stone pillars that flanked the shrines. Stones with carved heads were also found at Entremont, and those that appear on later Celtic pillar-stones and stone crosses are representations of the real heads that once graced Celtic settlements. A Celtic head is integral with the head of the cross at Trevean in St Erth parish, Cornwall. According to ancient Celtic belief, the head contains the essence of the individual, and, by preserving the head, this part of the soul remains present after death. Although it is of Pagan origin, the Celtic cult of the head did not cease in Ireland or Scotland with the advent of Christianity. Until the seventeenth century, it remained the common practice to behead all of those slain or captured in battle. Also the heads of famous priests and monks were preserved as relics. Many Celtic churches contain human skulls still. The cult is recalled by the remarkable panel on Clonfert Cathedral, which demonstrates the Pythagorean number system known as the *tetraktys* by means of ten stone heads set in a triangular panel.

TUMULUS STONES AND LEACHTA

In Pagan times, it was customary to set up large memorial stones on top of the grave-mounds of the high and mighty. The ensemble of the burial mound with a standing stone or image on top of it is the fore-runner of the Celtic high crosses, set upon their pyramidal or stepped bases. In Ireland, we can see other forerunners of the high crosses in the shape of the *leachta*. These are small rectangular drystone structures that resemble altars. On top of each *leacht* is a stone slab, often incised with crosses. Set into this is an upright stone cross, which is usually accompanied by large loose pebbles. These are used in votive rites of healing or cursing, being turned by the supplicants during prayers and invocations. The cross-slabs that stand on top of the *leachta* have much in common with the pillar-stones that stood on the Celtic burial-places in Pagan times. Furthermore, the Irish word *leacht* is derived from the Latin, *lectus*, meaning a bed, which is a name often gives to graves in Celtic countries. Naturally, because they are holy, no *leachta* have been excavated to see whether anyone is buried beneath them. Like crosses, *leachta* are holy stopping-places at which prayers are offered by devout people. Some sacred enclosures have a number of them, each of which has a slightly different character. For example, the island of Inishmurray in County Sligo has eleven *leachta*, which are used as stopping-places in ceremonial processions during religious festivals. It is likely that the erection of *leachta* was formerly widespread in Celtic countries, and that the enormous calvaries of Brittany that were erected much later are a development of them.

The custom of erecting a memorial stone on top of a burial mound was widespread in ancient European Paganism. We can have some idea of how they looked in former times if we visit the places in the *Land* of Baden-Württemberg in southern Germany where a number of Celtic mounds have been reconstructed. Among the mounds with new stones are those at Hochdorf, Echterdingen and Hohmichele. Unfortunately, there is too little information available as to how the stones were painted originally, or how the rings of posts that surrounded the mounds were carved.

The custom of erecting a memorial stone on top of a burial mound was widespread in ancient European Paganism.

However, many Celtic mounds have been excavated, and we are fortunate that modern archaeology has recovered the splendour of some of the burials that lay beneath the mounds. The exquisite artefacts excavated from the burials of a wealthy woman at Vix in France and a high-class man at Hochdorf reflect every aspect of Celtic spirituality. In the artefacts from these and other burials we can see actual representations of themes recorded later in the Celtic spiritual literature of Ireland and Britain. They recall the ensouled world of Celtic tradition, in which every artefact is not merely an object but possesses its own unique personality.

Each thing, made a by a Celtic craftsperson specially according to spiritual principles, contains within itself multiple meanings. The interchangeable forms of Celtic art express the plurality of existence, the multifaceted experiences of life, death and rebirth. Each type of artefact reflects its own symbolic qualities and mythic traditions which to this day continue to inspire contemporary Celtic art and spirituality. On both memorial stones and crosses, the patterns of Celtic art fade imperceptibly from one form into another, yet they always retain the same essence. Each Celtic artefact, from the largest stone to the smallest coin, expresses different aspects of this essential continuity, in which the forms of this material world and the otherworldly realm of spirit interpenetrate one another. According to the Celtic worldview, the realms of animals and humans, goddesses and gods, life and death are not separate. They are aspects of a great integrated continuum, in which everything is an aspect of the whole. According to the ancient maxim, 'as above, so below', in the Celtic worldview the structure of the greater world is reflected in the lesser. This is expressed in Celtic art, whose principles reflect the basic way that nature is structured. Each carved piece of wood or stone, each torc, ring and metal fitment, however small, is a perfect instance of this principle, which

According to the ancient maxim, 'as above, so below', in the Celtic worldview the structure of the greater world is reflected in the lesser.

was not destroyed when the Christian religion was introduced, but was nurtured and developed. Thus, the spirit of Celtic art was maintained within the Celtic church, and continued to underpin the newer Celtic culture without compromising its fundamental principles.

4
THE SIGNS OF THE LAND

Tattooing is an ancient means of permanently identifying one-self. Its origins are lost in antiquity, but it has been used in Europe for over 5,000 years. 'Ötzi', a man found frozen in the Austrian Alps in 1991, and dating from around 3300 BCE, had a cross tattooed on his left knee and other signs composed of dots and lines elsewhere. Two and a half thousand years later, geometric hand-tattoos are depicted in eighth-century BCE bronzes found at Kröll-Schmied-Kogel at Kleinklein in Steiermark, Austria. According to Herodotus, in the fifth century BCE the brave and renowned Scythian warriors were tattooed, and their tombs at Bashadar, Pazyryk, Shibe and Tuekta in the High Altai region of Siberia have yielded embalmed and frozen bodies preserved well enough to show what these tattoos were like. Known Scythian tattoo motifs include beaked horses, rams, lions, fish and plants. Many Scythian beasts are depicted with spirals at the joints in the manner of the later Celtic animal artwork.

PERSONAL SYMBOLS IN ANCIENT EUROPE

There are historic links between the Celts and the Scythians, and Scythian elements appear in the early Celtic art of the La Tène period. During the same period, aristocratic Thracian women were being tattooed. Thracian priestesses of Dionysos are shown with their tattoos on fifth-century BCE Greek vases. Later, the sword-wielding woman attacking the bull on the base of the Celtic-influenced Gundestrup Cauldron (first century BCE) is depicted with tattoos similar to those of Thracian priestesses. In the first century BCE, Julius Caesar reported that the Britons painted themselves with blue woad, and this may refer to tattoos as well as war-paint. The Lindow Man, whose body was pre-served in a bog, was tattooed, and the Picts were famed for the tattoos that they wore. Writing around the year 600, Isidore of Seville tells that the Picts were so called because their bodies were covered with pictures pricked into their skin using needles and coloured with herbs. The Celtic warriors' custom of fighting naked may in part have been intended to show off their body tattoos which served both to identify the warrior and to demonstrate his exploits.

We may have an idea of what Celtic tattoos looked like. Celtic coins found in the Channel Islands show that some Celts wore tattoos on the cheeks. The face of the sun god or Gorgo that once graced the pediment of the Celto-Roman temple at Bath has lines that may reproduce tattoos. Also, the grid markings on the Celto-Ligurian image from Roqueperteuse has already been mentioned, while a Gaulish Celtic stone image from Euffigneix, in Haute-Marne, France, dating from the first century BCE, depicts a man wearing a torc. On his body is an image of a boar, the sacred beast of the god Teutates, and an eye, symbol of Taranis. The Celtic custom of depicting symbols of the gods on the body is recorded in the histories of St Kentigern. In his mission to the Cumbrians in what is now Scotland, St Kentigern condemned those people who 'disfigured' their faces and bodies with tattoos in honour of the Pagan gods. Kentigern was following an edict of the Emperor Constantine (287–337), who forbade tattoos as a disfigurement of God's image in the human form.

Contemporary Irish churchmen, too, considered tattoos to be symbols or badges of Paganism, as opposed to the tonsure of Christian monks. Later, in the year 785, the Synod of Calcuth condemned the practice as un-Christian. The *Book of Kells*, written shortly afterwards, shows human figures with interlace, circle and point patterns on the body. The initial page of 'The Gospel According to St Mark' is a good example. Perhaps by this time, the artwork was influenced by the Coptic church, whose members were tattooed with fishes, crosses and other Christian emblems to identify themselves as irrevocably Christian. Later Celtic works do not depict humans in this way, for the practice of tattooing was proscribed in the British Isles, and those who had had them were dead.

Part of the arm-tattoos of a Scythian horseman, from a frozen tomb at Pazyryk in the High Altai Region, Siberia, preserved in the Hermitage Museum, St Petersburg. The treatment of horses, fish and other beasts in Scythian tattoos appears to be related to that of Celtic art.

OPPOSITE: The striking gorgoneion from the tympanum of the temple of Sulis Minerva at Bath, Avon, western England, showing syncretism between the Celtic and Roman traditions. The lines on the forehead of the solar being may recall the sacred tattoos of Celtic Paganism.

To the Pagan Celts, the multivalent deities could be symbolized both by aniconic and iconic images and by animals that embodied their character and power. In former times, it was the custom of the Celts to ally themselves with these animal powers in both warfare and spirituality. According to 'The Life of St Ciaran' (*The Lives of the British Saints*, Honourable Society of Cymmrodorion, 1908), the Irish monk's first disciples were a boar, a fox, a badger, a wolf and a doe. This does not mean that he was some kind of early St Francis of Assisi; rather it expressed the family allegiances of his human followers. Thus, he had a disciple whose name was Torc, the boar. Another, St Sinnach, came from the Hy Sinnach, or Fox, clan, from Teffa. His badger disciple was a member of the Broc tribe in Munster, while the wolf was Ciaran's uncle, Laighniadh Faeladh, whose epithet means both 'hospitable' and 'wolfish'. Finally, the doe, whose Irish name is Os, refers to a pupil who came to him from the people of Ossory. Each of these animals was emblematical of the tribe, being also a manifestation in animal form of the tribal goddess or god.

Thus, it is quite possible that Pictish symbol-stones reproduce the tattoos that were on the body of the person whom they commemorated. It is clear that the Christian church made a successful attempt to suppress the practice of tattooing, because it was Pagan. The Pictish king became Christian in the year 710. Then, cross-slabs began to supersede the earlier picture-stones and the Pictish symbols were subordinated to the cross, finally being relegated to the back of the stones. As the practice of tattooing died out, and Latin writing was introduced, perhaps there was no longer the need or indeed the possibility to identify an individual by his or her tattoos.

However, individual signs did not die out. Though their Pagan connections may have faded, they have continued until the present as the totems and

A Pictish slab from Papil, bearing images related to ancient tattoo-patterns. (*Historic Scotland*)

heraldic devices of clans and families. A poem in the *Book of Leinster*, entitled 'The Battle of Magh Rath', copied from an earlier manuscript by Finn MacGorman, who died in 1160, recalls the noble battle banners of ancient Celtic heraldry.

Mightily advance the battalions of Congal,
To us over the ford of Ornamh.
When they came to the contest of the men
They require not to be harangued.
The token of the great warrior of Macha,
The banner of the bright king with prosperity,
Over his own head conspicuously displayed,
The banner of Scandan – an ornament with prosperity,
And of Fiacha Mor, the standard of Baedan,
Great symbol of plunder floating from its staff,
Is over the head of Congal advancing towards us.
A yellow lion on green satin, the insignia of Craebh Ruadh,
Such as the noble Conchobar bore,
Is now held up by Congal.
The standards of the host of Eochaidh
Before the embattled hosts,
Are dun-coloured standards like fire
Over the well-shaped spear-handles of Crumthann.
The standard of the vigorous king of Britain,
Conan Rod, the royal soldier,
Streaked satin, blue and white,
In folds displayed.
The standard of the great king of Saxonland of hosts
Is a wide, very great standard,
Yellow and red, richly displayed.
Over the head of Dairble, son of Dornmor
The standard of the major king of Feabhail
(I have not seen such another),
Is over his head (no treachery does he carry with him),
Black and red, Cent.
The standard of Suibhne – a yellow banner,
The renowned king of Dal Ariadhe,
Yellow satin, over that mild man of hosts,
The white-fingered stripling himself in the midst of them.
The standard of Feroman of Banquets,
The red-weaponed king of the Ards of Ulster,
White satin, to the sun and wind displayed,
Over that mighty man without blemish.

This poem described, for those who did not know it, the heraldry of the monarchs of the British Isles. It is not inconceivable that such consecrated battle-standards were reproduced on commemorative stones, which originally were painted in the appropriate colours. The tattoos that people wore on their bodies, their tribal, clan and family emblems, colours and heraldry are linked intimately to the landscape from which they come. They are as much a part of the land as the rivers and hills, fields and track-ways, villages and holy places that make up the traditional landscape of northern Europe. Standing stones and stone crosses do not exist separately from the landscape in which they stand. They are important landmarks in their own right, often bearing their own names which tell something of their history and meaning. Thus, stones and crosses are repositories of the local spir-it of place, preserving and expressing the particular character of the land of which they are part. Crosses are always stopping-places in the landscape, places on pathways where travellers can rest, pray and restore body and spirit before going on their way. In difficult terrain, crosses mark the way, showing the wayfarer the most favourable path between villages or monasteries.

Standing stones and stone crosses do not exist separately from the landscape in which they stand. They are important landmarks in their own right, often bearing their own names which tell something of their history and meaning.

NAMING THE LAND

In early days of Christianity, it was customary for missionaries to set up preaching-stations at stopping-places on trackways, in markets or at other locations where people passed by or gathered together. These holy stopping-places where the priest offered prayers and preached the gospel were marked by a standing cross. This could be either a portable processional staff-cross temporarily put into the ground during sacred activities, and removed afterwards, in the manner of a maypole, or a permanent cross of some kind. When the missionary priest died, his followers would bury him at one of these stopping-places, creating further layers of sanctity upon an already hallowed place. Such standing crosses were used for outdoor services in places where there was no church. In the sixth century, the Roman Emperor Justinian ordered that the erection of a cross should precede the building of a church, and the consecration ceremony for churchyards involved the erection of a wooden cross on the boundary at each of the four cardinal directions. A cross could serve as a place of worship where there was no church, as recorded in 'The Life of St Willibald' (*The Lives of the British Saints*, Honourable Society of Cymmrodorion, 1908), which tells that Saxon land-owners erected crosses at which daily worship was held, in preference to far more expensive churches.

Pilgrimage, the spiritual journey in which the devotee travels in a prayerful, meditative way to a holy place, has always played an important part in religion. Although making a pilgrimage to the Holy Land or Rome was considered good for Christian souls, in practical terms this was rarely possible. As an inferior substitute for the real thing, local pilgrimages and sacred circuits or 'rounds' were undertaken. Walking prayerfully around a relatively small area, the pilgrim visited a number of holy places in a certain order. These places were often marked by crosses. Whether a sacred circuit was around a churchyard, through a town, or around a whole parish, it would take only a day at most to complete. Visiting each cross or other holy stopping-place in turn, the pilgrim said appropriate prayers and offered oblations at each one. Today, sometimes, rounds are undertaken on the local saint's day. In Britanny, this ceremony is known as a Pardon, while in Ireland it is called the saint's Pattern or Patron. At such events, pilgrims experience a progressive heightening of their religious experience through the medium of the geomythic landscape.

A typical Cornish wayside cross on the verge of a lane near Tintagel, Cornwall. *(Nigel Pennick)*

In England, the holy stopping-places on the monastic trackway across Dartmoor between Tavistock Abbey and Buckfast Abbey in Devon are marked by a particularly well-preserved series of named crosses. The first cross after leaving Tavistock Abbey is Green Lane Cross. Then come Pixies' Cross, Warren's Cross, Huckworthy Cross, Walkhampton Church House Cross and Yannandon Cross. The trackway takes wayfarers on to Lower Lowery Cross, then to Lowery Cross, and across Lether Tor Bridge to Clazywell Cross. Next come

Newleycombe Cross, Siward's Cross, Nun's Cross, Goldsmith's Cross and Childe's Tomb Cross. Then, the difficult terrain is marked and sanctified by Mount Misery Cross, which leads us on to West Ter Hill Cross, then East Ter Hill Cross, and to the river crossing-place at Skaur Ford Cross. The next crossing-place is protected by Horse Ford Cross, from which the trackway takes us to Horn's Cross, then via Two Thorns Cross, Play Cross and Hawson Cross to Buckfast Abbey. Thus, the entire trackway is marked and made holy by the crosses that serve as waymarkers and spiritual support for the wayfarer. In East Anglia, crosses waymarked the pilgrimage routes to the shrine of Our Lady at Walsingham, one of the major shrines of medieval Britain.

Another series of crosses is associated with Aldhelm of Malmesbury, who died in the year 709. The Wiltshire monastery of Malmesbury was founded by Maeldubh, an Irishman, and Celtic traditions prevailed there under the rule of the West Saxons. According to legend, St Aldhelm was born in a churchyard at the foot of a standing cross, becoming in due course a noted prelate of the church. After a long life of founding new churches and doubtless setting up crosses, Aldhelm died at Doulting in the house of his Pagan friend, Kenred. His body was borne back to Malmesbury in solemn procession from Doulting. The cortège took a circuitous ceremonial route which involved seven stages of seven miles a day. Later, stone crosses were erected at the stopping-places where the cortège had halted. Fragments of cross at Bath Abbey, Colerne and Littleton Drew are said to be their remnants.

In Celtic tradition, there is no hard-and-fast rule that divides mythology from history. Although they are frequently dismissed as having originated in attempts by primitive poets to explain the unknown, myths nevertheless contain primordial truths. They are not intended to be taken literally, for they exist outside physical reality in the realm of metaphor. In order to understand their inner nature, we must take these myths on their own terms, neither dismissing them as meaningless fantasies nor rationalizing them. It is possible to interpret any landscape

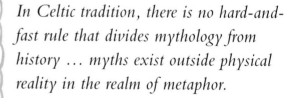

In Celtic tradition, there is no hard-and-fast rule that divides mythology from history ... myths exist outside physical reality in the realm of metaphor.

myth in a number of different ways, each of which may prove insightful. Essentially, our approach to such myths and legends is individual and personal. Throughout the sacred landscape of the British Isles and

Brittany, the names of crosses, and the stories told about them, weave a geomythic fabric of the land which expresses its character in a particular way. So, in Brittany, the cross at the place called La Croix des Sept Chemins, where seven roads meet, marks the spot where seven brothers (Connec, Dardanaou, Gerna, Gonery, Jort, Merhé and Quidec) embraced and left to preach the gospel. All of them became saints in the Celtic church, for each founded a chapel in the direction in which he went. Through the Celtic Cross, following on from the earlier Pagan stone, ancestral heritage is maintained and the mythic spirit of the landscape lives through those who experience it.

Celtic tradition celebrates multiplicity. Its mythology is full of events that take place at a certain place through the coming-together of a number of unrelated causes, each of which could cause the event alone. Integrating unrelated things into a coherent whole is one of the arts of the Celtic bard. The Irish wizard Bec mac Dé is reputed to have been able to hear nine separate questions from nine different people at one time, and to respond to them with a single answer. Similarly, the Celtic Cross, with its origins in many different sacred areas, is the point of coincidence that reflects the Celtic principle of unity in multiplicity.

In traditional Celtic society, there was nothing impersonal. Each thing that a man or woman encountered in everyday living had its own life, too. Each thing was a subject, not an object, which could be spoken of by its own, personal, name. This was because every natural thing, human artefact and part of the landscape was named. Each name reflected some inner nature, a personal quality that had meaning. In the ensouled Celtic worldview, the personality of every place and artefact was recognized to be as real as the individual personalities of human beings. This is the case with seemingly inanimate objects such as stones and crosses. Such an ensouled world can only exist when there is intimate personal contact with existence. When individual things are made by craftspeople, then no two are the same, but once manufacturing industry arose, with mass-production of multiple things, then the personal contact was lost. Artefacts became anonymous products, whose essential character no longer originated in the individual character of its maker and users. Today, many of the names of the landscape are lost or forgotten, or overlain by meaningless inventions. The naming of the world has continued in a few specialized areas, such as in the names of private and public houses, hotels, aircraft and ships. On a smaller level, it is even less frequent, with the occasional exception of particularly personal possessions such as cars, knives, guns and guitars.

5
HEAVENLY COLUMNS

The Celtic Cross has a number of antecedents, all of which have contributed their particular qualities. Places where paths and trackways join, especially crossroads, are marked in every culture as special spiritual places somehow different from the rest of the world. According to cosmic symbolism, the crossroads is the place where the cosmic axis between the underworld and the upperworld intersects with middle earth. Spiritually, the crossroads is a place where the distinction between the physical plane and the non-material worlds is less certain. In ancient Greece and Rome, crossroads were marked with an ithyphallic pillar-image of Hermes (Mercury), god of the crossways and psychopomp of the dead. Known as a *Herm*, frequently the pillar was sheltered by a tree and accompanied by an altar upon which travellers made offerings.

Crossroads were significant places in ancient Celtic culture. In his account of the Gauls, Julius Caesar stated that the chief god of the Celts was: 'Mercury, of whom there are many images throughout Gaul: he is considered to be the originator of all of the arts; the god who indicates the right road and guides the traveller's footsteps; he is the great patron of trade and riches.' The god about whom Caesar wrote has the attributes of the Irish god Lugh. In places influenced by Germanic and Scandinavian Paganism, the crossroads was a holy place of the god of commerce and interchange, Woden, who was also the god of hanged men. Thus, in the north, the crossroads were especially sacred to the dead, being a place where, at certain times, it was possible to commune with departed spirits. When the Christian religion was introduced, the sacred cross of roads was re-interpreted naturally as being symbolic of the cross of Christ, at which priests erected stone crosses that served as stopping-places for wayfarers and pilgrims.

In the present-day German province of Westphalia, outside the Roman Empire, the Pagan Saxons had a sacred column as the focus of their religious devotions. It stood at a holy place called the Eresburg, occupied today by the medieval parish church of the town of Ober-Marsberg. The Latin text, called *Translatio S. Alexandri*, tells how the Saxons venerated it as a: 'large wooden column set up in the open. In their language it is called *Irminsul*, which in Latin is a "universal column".' Like the *omphalos*, *Irminsul* is a symbol of eternal stability at the centre of a changing world. It is the everlasting 'tree of measure' planted by the grand geometer of the universe, an earthly emblem of the deity. The sacred pillar of the Eresburg was felled in the year 772 on the orders of the Emperor Charlemagne as a symbol of his conquest of the Saxons. According to the historian Widukind, *Irminsul* and similar pillars were sacred to Mars, and they were located at places that represented the sun. The placename of Ober-Marsberg echoes this sacred connection. After Charlemagne, similar columns were erected in Saxony, but instead of having a Pagan meaning they were in honour of the Christian hero, Roland. The form of *Irminsul*, a column with a volute capital, later reappeared in Christian art as the lower part of many Celtic Crosses.

THE MAYPOLE

The general principle of the heavenly column appears to be very ancient, seemingly going back at least 3,000 years. A remarkable pointed conical golden object called a *goldkegel* found at Ezelsdorf, near Nuremberg, and dating from 1100 BCE, is believed to be the top of such a pillar. Also, from the evidence of enormous post-holes, it appears that votive posts were erected in the Celtic sacred enclosures favoured in Germany and France. In more recent times, maypoles have been set up each year to celebrate the Celtic festival of Beltane. The custom was formerly widespread throughout northern Europe, but its use has dwindled in the British Isles. A visit to southern Germany on Mayday is recommended for readers who want some idea of what maypole festivities were like in former times in Celtic countries. We know of the customs from relatively recent records, but there is no reason to suggest that they were not substantially the same in ancient times. Indeed, during the Reformation, Protestants pointed out their Pagan origin and condemned them as such, and that was the end of the Maytide celebrations in many places. However, this view of folk-culture is needlessly harsh and rigid. To most participants in any folk festival, the religious component is less important than the enjoyment it brings. The great Mardi Gras carnivals of New Orleans and Rio de Janeiro, ostensibly commemorating the beginning of the fast period of Lent, are perfect examples of this.

In former times, the Welsh maypole was a birch tree, as it is in some parts of Germany today. In his *Crefydd yr Oesoedd Tywyll* (1852), the bard Nefydd (William Roberts) left an account of Welsh traditions of *Codi'r Fedwen* (raising the birch), which was accompanied by the *dawns y fedwen* (the dance of the birch), a kind of morris dancing. 'The May-pole was prepared by painting it in different colours,' wrote Nefydd, 'then the leader of the dance would come and place his circle of ribbon about the pole, and each in his turn after him, until the May-pole was all ribbons from one end to the other. Then it was raised into position and the dance begun.' Dancing around the pole was the main activity of Mayday. In some localities, a number of poles were set up close to one another. They created a 'round' of stopping-places which were visited in order by the revellers in the manner of the pilgrims' crosses at holy places. Until the nineteenth century, people of Tenby in Pembrokeshire would set up a number of maypoles in the town on Mayday. They were used as stopping-places for a round-dance of the town. An account of 1858 tells us that 'May-poles were reared up in different parts of the town, decorated with flowers, coloured papers, and bunches of variegated ribbon. On May-day, the young men and maidens would, joining hand

This English permanent maypole on the village green at Wellow, Nottinghamshire, is painted spirally with the national colours of red, white and blue, and bears the solar emblem of a gilded weathercock at the summit. *(Nigel Pennick)*

in hand, dance round the May-poles and "thread the needle".... A group from fifty to 100 persons would wend their way from one pole to another, till they had traversed the town ....' In some places, similar poles were also erected to mark midsummer. *Y fedwen haf*, the summer birch, was erected in the Vale of Glamorgan on St John's Day, 24 June. Similar to the maypole, the summer birch was garlanded before the dancers circled it.

JUPITER COLUMNS

Another forerunner of the Celtic cross is the Jupiter Column. As a type of monument, it seems that Jupiter Columns came into being as the result of a remarkable incident. In 65 BCE, the image of Jupiter at the Capitol in Rome was destroyed by a lightning strike, along with stone tablets of the law and a statue of one of the twins beneath the Roman wolf. The destruction of some of the most sacred images of Rome was recognized as a disastrous omen for Roman society and the future of the city. Official investigations were put in hand to determine the nature of the threat, and a means to avert it. Whether the original, destroyed image of Jupiter had been set upon a column is uncertain, but, after Etruscan *haruspices* had investigated the omens, the augurs decided to set up a column to Jupiter on the site of the previous image. This was erected ceremonially in 63 BCE, with an image of the god watching over his people. To the Romans, Jupiter, father of the gods and the people, was the great architect of the universe, sustainer of all. The architectural column is thus completely appropriate as a symbol of the god. As protector of the city, the new column became the model for others in the western Roman Empire. Outside Italy, Jupiter Columns are found in the Celtic realms that came under Roman rule. While they are known from Britain, Brittany and most of France, the vast majority of columns have been discovered in Lorraine and Alsace and the Rhineland region of Germany, where the remains of 300 have been identified.

Most Jupiter Columns follow an iconic programme. At the base of the typical Jupiter Column is a four-sided stone pedestal carved as a so-called 'four-god stone'. Generally, this consists of four images of divine beings: two female and two male. A common scheme has the goddess Juno on the front side; Minerva on the right side; Hercules on the rear; and Mercury on the left. Sometimes Mercury is replaced by Apollo, while a column from Hausen has an eagle bearing an inscription on the front side. On the left of the eagle is Apollo; the back bears Diana, and the right completes the four-deity scheme with an image of Venus and Vulcan. Some columns have an inscription carved on the front side of the base. Above this pedestal stands a seven- or eight-sided part with divine images. Usually, they depict the goddesses and gods of the days of the week, though some columns depart from this scheme. When the days of the week are personified, the eighth place is occupied usually by a dedication or an image of Victoria, the goddess of victory. This so-called 'seven-god stone' part supports the shaft of the column. The deities carved on this section seem to have been more variable than those on the base. While a column found at Plieningen, in the Stuttgart region, has only the weekday images of Saturn, Sol, Luna, Mars, Mercury, Jupiter and Venus, another, found at Schwaigern-Stetten, in the region of Heilbronn, has carvings of Sol, Luna, Vesta, Neptune, Mercury and Maia Rosmerta.

From this seven- or eight-fold stone comes the shaft, which in many cases is carved with patterns. Sometimes the patterns resemble the bark of a tree. A variation can be seen on a Jupiter Column from Hausen which is covered with stylized oak leaves and acorns in a regular tesselation. The oak was the holy tree of Jupiter and his sky-god equivalents in the other European pantheons. Typical of Jupiter Column shafts is one discovered at Walheim, which has the lower portion resembling scales or bark, while the upper portion, divided from it by a ropelike pattern, has a vinescroll in which human figures carry out various

Originally associated with Dionysos, the vinescroll was adopted by the Christian artists to become a major element in their iconography, re-interpreted as 'the true vine' ... Jesus Christ.

actions. Originally associated with Dionysos, the vinescroll was adopted by the Christian artists to become a major element in their iconography, re-interpreted as 'the true vine', signifying the regenerative powers symbolized by Jesus Christ. Closely following the example of Jupiter Columns, scrolls of vine leaves appear on the shafts of Celtic Crosses. Good examples exist at Penally in west Wales and on many crosses that originated in the old Anglian kingdoms of Northumbria and Mercia in England, where Roman influence was strong.

There is another variant type of Jupiter Column which has the figures of the goddesses and gods on the shaft. Two of this type are known from the German city of Mainz alone. The larger of the two

The reconstructed Roman Jupiter Column that stands in the city centre of Stuttgart, Baden-Württemberg, Germany. (*Nigel Pennick*)

has been reconstructed, without Jupiter on top, and stands in the Mainzer Deutschhausplatz. The other had the figures of the goddesses and gods on the shaft, superimposed on a bark- or scalelike pattern. Above the columnar part is the capital that supports the image of Jupiter himself. The capital is composed of conventional foliage, but often it is carved with four heads that represent the four seasons, looking outwards to the four quarters. Finally, on top of the column is the image of the god. Often, he is depicted on horseback or in a chariot, riding down a humanoid yet demonic figure, which has serpents in place of legs. Terrified, the victim falls beneath the rampant hooves. In his right hand, the triumphant Jupiter holds a thunderbolt. Alternatively, the god is seated on a throne. Several surviving Jupiter Columns in Germany also depict him as the god with the wheel. On the column fragment at Butterstadt, the mounted Jupiter carries a wheel as a shield, while the column at Alzey has a wheel on the side of Jupiter's throne.

Symbolically, Jupiter Columns are a summation of time and space, and the Roman pantheon. Later, when Christianity had superseded Paganism as the state religion, this scheme of portraying the gods and goddesses on a column was taken up by churchmen and interpreted according to the newer doctrines. The Celtic Crosses that bear images of the figures of the three-fold godhead, prophets, patriarchs and saints are a re-interpretation of the scheme of the Pagan Jupiter Columns. The classical column was too good a symbolic form to abandon. The fantastic baroque *Pestsäule* and *Lichtsäule* of Austria are other instances of this re-interpretation at a later date. Erected in the eighteenth century, they often depict Our Lady's ascent into heaven amid an entourage of angels, putti and saints.

THE GOTLAND MEMORIAL STONES

Before the year 400, the Pagan people of the Baltic island of Gotland, now part of Sweden, set up unhewn stone slabs, without, as far as is known, sculpture or other ornament. Around the year 400, however, there was a change, and people began to set up larger and more ornate stones. These were generally rectangular in shape, with painted images and symbols. Further progression in stone design produced monuments with horseshoe-shaped tops, and interlace pattern around the edges, in the manner of later Pictish cross-slabs. These date from the sixth century onwards. Prominent on many Gotland stones is the disc or wheel. Some depict it in the form of a dynamic whirling pattern, as on the stone from Sanda illustrated here, while others are more wheel-like. The Sanda disc is composed of eight light crescents interspersed with eight others made from alternate light and dark triangles. Other discs are divided into four by lines or spirals. The pattern on stones from

OPPOSITE: Gotland memorial stones.
Centre: a painted stone from Sanda, whose roundel occupies the same place as the wheel-cross on comparable Christian stones.
Left (descending): border from Hablingo Havor; border from Vallstena; roundel from Vallstena; roundel from Hablingo Havor.
Right (descending): border from Hablingo Havor; border from Larbro St Hammers; roundels from Västkünde Björkome.

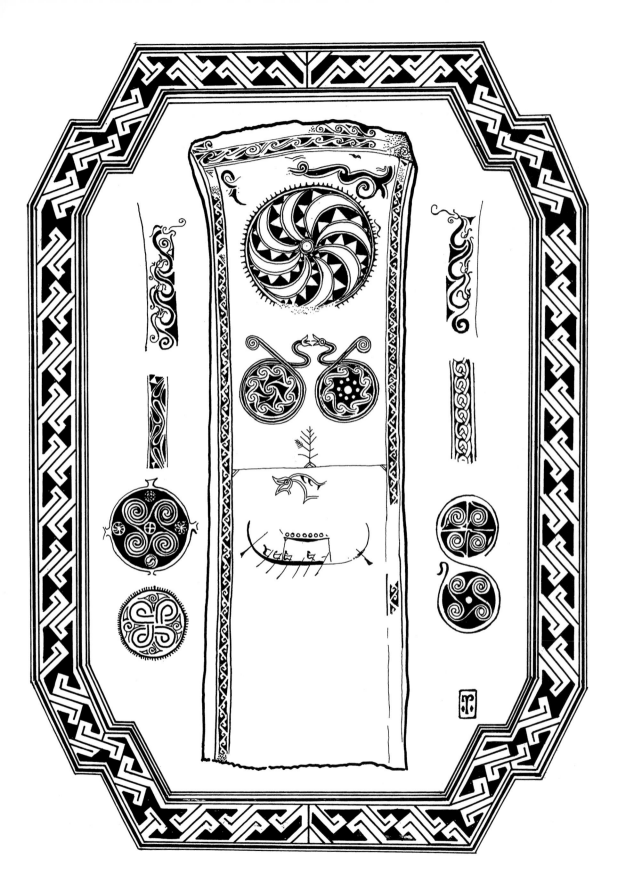

Martebo, Vallstena and Västkünde Björkome have clear affinities with the sunwheel and the Celtic Cross. An alternative form is the knot-wheel, such as that on a stone from Hablingo Havor, examples of which are found on later runestones and Celtic Crosses. The position of the centres of the spirals and the 'holes' in the knot of the knotwheel are identical with the holes, real or inferred, that are the characteristic of the design of Celtic Crosses. Furthermore, the position of the disc on the Gotland stones is identical with that of the wheel-cross on early Celtic cross-slabs. The meaning of these stylistic concurrences between the Baltic and the British Isles has yet to be determined.

The border ornament of Gutnish stones (see the examples on page 57) varies from running spirals through swirl-patterns to interlace identical in form to that found on Celtic artefacts. It is possible that these bordered patterns reproduce tapestry patterns in stone, for the use of tapestries and hangings in a sacred context is universal. They are known from Celtic burials as far back as the La Tène era. Surviving northern-tradition tapestries, such as the twelfth-century one from Skog church, Hälsingland, Sweden, show the pantheon in iconic form. The style and content of Roman, Coptic and Byzantine tapestries may have had an influence upon northern European styles of presentation, Gutnish memorial-stones of the Sanda type, and Pictish cross-slabs, such as that at Rossie Priory in Tayside, may be images in stone of fabric sacred hangings, now lost. More enigmatic is their relationship with the much earlier Etruscan funerary stelae of Italy. Dating from the fourth century BCE, these memorial stones have many pictorial themes carved within scrolled borders which artistically are close to both the Gutnish and Pictish stones.

RUNESTONES

It was a convention in northern Europe in early medieval times to portray the cosmic axis in the form of *Irminsul*, which was represented as a column with a top composed of interlace patterns or opposed scrolls. Perhaps this was in imitation of classical columns or the middle-eastern palm tree of life from which those columns were derived. The axis of *Irminsul* sometimes resembles the lower part of a Celtic Cross, without the head. This has both a stylistic and a symbolic meaning because the same form was used frequently by Celtic crossmakers, both as the transition point between the cross-shaft and its head and also as additional ornament. In the days before the literalism of the witch-hunts and the

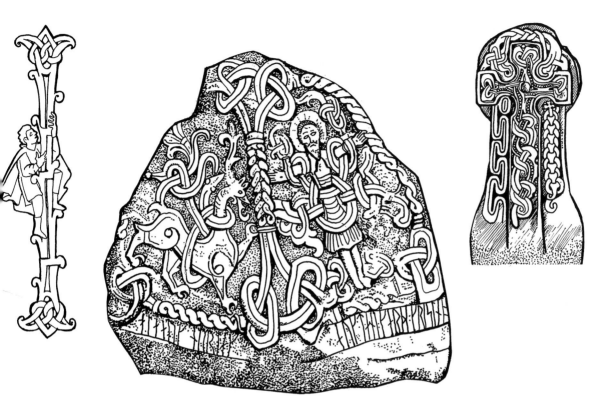

Irminsul.
Left: a drawing from an illuminated manuscript of the Reichenau School, tenth century, showing a man climbing the cosmic axis *Irminsul.*
Centre: the runestone of King Harald Bluetooth at Jelling, Denmark, depicts Christ and the bound Fenris-Wolf flanking *Irminsul.*
Right: Celtic Cross at Ballaugh, Isle of Man, in the form of *Irminsul.*

Reformation, many believers recognized that the Christian religion was a continuation and a refinement of the elder faith rather than its inflexible enemy. The integration of *Irminsul* with the cross was therefore a natural progression, where a cross-head was simply added to the top of the cosmic axis.

Irminsul itself appears in Christian art as a representation of Jacob's Ladder, linking earth and heaven. A tenth-century Christian manuscript of the Reichenau School kept at the Herzog August Bibliothek in Wolfenbüttel actually shows a man climbing up *Irminsul*. It is an image of the soul's ascent from earth to heaven. The great eleventh-century runestone at Jelling in Denmark, erected by King Harald, has both the crucifixion and *Irminsul*. It shows Christ crucified and bound with interlacing ribbonwork. Beside him, carved on the edges of the stone, are twin representations of *Irminsul*, resembling that on the Wolfenbüttel manuscript. Thus, the Pagan cosmic axis reflects its Christian counterpart in the cross, integrating the older and newer sacred cosmologies. Many Scandinavian runestones used the *Irminsul* form for the presentation of the runic inscription. Conventionally, the script began at the bottom of the stone, and read upwards along the

59

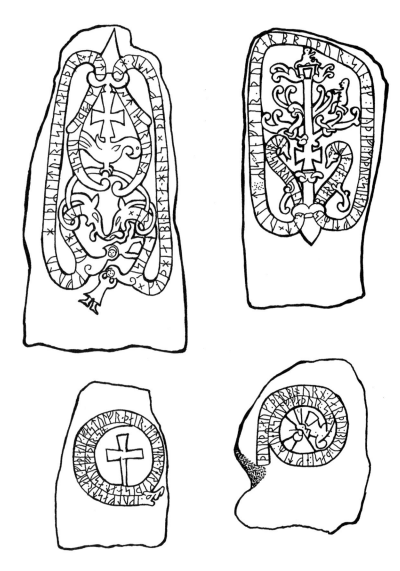

Swedish runestones, with runic inscriptions carved inside the *lindwurm* serpent, incorporating Pagan and Christian motifs.
Clockwise from top left:
Grynsta Backe, Tible, Upland; Årsunde parish, Gestrike; Glömsiö bridge, Börke, Småland; Hesle, Eggeby, Upland.

stem of the axis to its top. Then, if the script was longer, it continued downwards to the right of the axis, effectively in a sunwise spiral, until it reached the bottom of the stone. Further text was written upwards to the left of the axis. Other runestones depict the Tree of Life at the centre of scrolls that bear the runes. In these images, artistic elements integrate *Irminsul*, the cross and the Hammer of Thor to produce unique designs. Finally, there is a form that puts the runes in a spiral serpentine ribbon that coils around a Christian cross, making the sun-wheel pattern.

6

EARLY CELTIC CROSSES

The Celtic Cross did not evolve out of nothing, or even as the development of a single precursor. As we have seen, it is a syncretic structure that came into being under a particular set of conditions as the result of an accumulation of ideas, symbols and traditions. In its most basic form, the cross itself was not originally Christian, nor was it used openly in the earliest years of the Christian religion. Before it was adopted as an exclusively Christian sign in the year 680, the cross was a symbol of land-measure, employed by diviners and the *agrimensores*, members of the Roman guild of surveyors. In his *De Divinatione*, Cicero, who was an augur, tells that in his time the staff carried by the Roman augurs was in the form of a cross. As time passed, however, the generally sacred symbol of the cross gradually developed a more specific, Christian meaning.

Images close to the later Celtic Cross existed in the Coptic church. A good example can be seen in the Coptic manuscript known as the *Codex Brucianus*. Preserved in the Bodleian Library at Oxford, it has an illuminated cover in the form of an ornamented ankh-cross. In Egyptian religious iconography, the ankh or *crux ansata* was the symbol for life. The Coptic Christians took the symbol and amalgamated it with the wheel and cross. The Coptic funerary stela from Armant near Luxor (see page 62) shows how they integrated the older Egyptian symbols for life with the newer Christian ones. Interestingly, the scribe of the *Codex Brucianus* has illuminated the ankh-cross with interlace patterns and tesselations that today are the epitome of the Celtic Cross.

THE SIGN OF THE CROSS

Like the ankh before it, the cross was invested with great power both to consecrate and to ward off harm. Writing in his *De Corona Militis*, at the end of the second century, Tertullian tells how the early Christians

used the cross as a universal protective gesture: 'At every commencement of business, whenever we go in or come out of any place, when we dress for a journey, when we go into a bath, when we go to meat, when lights are brought in, when we lie down or sit down, and whatever business we have, we make on our foreheads the sign of the cross.' When the Christians of that time wanted to signify Christ, however, they used symbols other than the cross. Most popular were the fish, the lamb, the good shepherd (taken from images of Apollo), the Greek letters *alpha* and *omega*, and the *chi-rho* monogram. This latter sign took a number of forms, the earliest of which was made with the Greek letters X (*chi*) and P (*rho*) as on the Coptic stela. Sometimes, the monogram was shown inside a circle or laurel wreath. In Britain, this earliest form of *chi-rho* exists in the floor mosaic from the Roman house at Hinton St Mary in Dorset, preserved in the British Museum.

By the late fourth century, there was the tendency to turn the X into an upright position, thereby converting the *chi-rho* into a looped-headed vertical cross. A good example of this type of *chi-rho* can be seen on a stone which is preserved inside the church at Penmachno in Gwynedd. Bearing a Latin inscription that reads (in translation) 'Carausius lies here in this cairn', the stone, which stood on a burial-cairn in continuation of Celtic Pagan tradition, has been dated to the late fifth or early sixth century. Above the inscription is a looped cross *chi-rho* without a surrounding circle. Around the late fifth century, Celtic carvers began to make sunwheel crosses with a right-facing hook in the upper arm. Finally, the hook or P was dropped, and a cross in a circle was the result. Sometimes it was accompanied by the Greek letters *alpha* and *omega*, symbolizing the beginning and the end. A pillar-stone preserved in the chapel at Kirkmadrine in Galloway is a good example of such a hooked-head cross within a circle. It was not until the year 680 that the cross and related crucifix was adopted officially by the church at a General Council held in Constantinople, when at last a standardized form was agreed for Christian use.

An early cross-stone in the Carmarthen Museum collection is a stone taken from Castelldwyran in Dyfed, called 'The Memorial of Voteporix Protector'. It is a pointed megalith with inscriptions in Latin and ogham. Prominent above the inscription is a ring-cross or sun-wheel without any hook or P on the top arm. It is a characteristic form, for similar inscribed stones were erected in other parts of the British Isles at this time. In Ireland, there are numerous extant slabs carved with wheel-crosses composed of geometrically drawn arcs.

OPPOSITE: A Coptic tombstone from Armant near Luxor, Egypt, dating from around the year 400, carved with *chi-rho*, *alpha* and *omega*, crosses, ankhs and the Egyptian hieroglyph for 'union', denoting the continuity of Christianity with Paganism.

Although most of the arc-crosses have four arms, this number is not fixed. Some have six or seven arms. Perhaps these are not Christian monuments at all, but memorials of Pagans or those of dual faith. However, multiple-armed wheels appear on stones that are certainly Christian. A notable cross-slab at Maughold on the Isle of Man, dating from the late seventh or early eighth century, has as its main carving not a cross but a six-fold consecration-wheel of the kind common on Roman Pagan altars and associated with the goddess Juno. However, its Christian intent is without question, for the six-fold wheel is surrounded by an inscription dedicated to the bishop Irneit, carved in a circle in the manner of seals. Beneath it are two Latin crosses accompanied by texts.

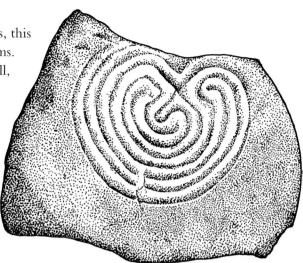

This labyrinth-inscribed boulder from Hollywood, Upper Lockstown, County Wicklow, now in the National Museum of Ireland in Dublin, marked a sacred stopping-place on the pilgrims' road leading to the holy place of St Kevin at Glendalough. When it was discovered, the labyrinth pattern was not recognized, and it was kept as a cross.

Although they are rare, certain Irish stones of this type survive because they are stopping-places on pilgrimage routes set up by early missionaries. In the valley of Glencolmkille in County Donegal is a series of cross-carved stones, set up on cairns at which present-day pilgrims pray like their forebears did. Other stones of this type mark the tracks to and on Mount Brandon, around Croagh Patrick, on Caher Island and at the pilgrimage centres of Ballyvourney, Clonmacnois and Glendalough. They can also be found outside Ireland, in Iona and the Shetland Isles.

MEGALITHIC CROSS-SLABS AND HOLED STONES

The cross-slab at the former monastery of Reask in County Kerry is of interest as a surviving bridge between the older and the newer forms of Celtic art. The carvings on the cross at Reask are comparable with patterns on Pagan stones from the La Tène Celtic culture in what is now south Germany. The Reask stone is irregular in shape, and the four-fold cross pattern cut into it has been squashed from a true circle to fit the asymmetrical megalith upon which it is carved. However, it is clear that there is a reason for this beyond laziness or incompetence. When one views the cross from a distance, it is apparent that the shape of its top imitates that of the distant horizon. This reflectivity of stone profile and horizon can be seen elsewhere in the British Isles. Some stone

RIGHT: Early Christian cross-slab at Reask (Riasc), County Kerry, Ireland.

BELOW: The cross-slab dedicated to Bishop Irneit, from Maughold, Isle of Man, carved with a six-fold Juno's Wheel below which are inscribed Latin crosses. *(Manx National Heritage)*

circles, most notably at Castlerigg in Cumbria, have this feature in almost every megalith. The Reask stone is clearly within this megalithic tradition. In addition to its horizon-following shape, it was also once pierced by a hole like many ancient magical megaliths, but this is now broken out. The practice of drilling holes through stones is archaic, and many ancient rockfaces and megaliths contain 'cup-marks' where people have made shallow depressions in the stone. Cup-marks are especially prevalent on sculpted stones such as those at Newgrange and other megalithic holy places. Although it cannot be stated for certain why the ancient cup-marks were made, more recent folk-tradition shows that it was customary to scrape away dust from holy stones for use as a medicinal remedy.

Cup-marks are found on stones in the fabric of churches and crosses as well as upon archaic megaliths. A number of Cornish cross-shafts are covered with drilled-out holes, such as that in the old churchyard of Merthyr Uny, in the parish of St Wendron. Other Cornish crosses have a depression at the centre of the wheel-head where a boss might be. Crosses like this exist or have existed at Bodmin, Callyworth, Crowan, Clowance, Lanteglos and St Kew. In addition to these depressions, a number of extant Celtic stones have holes drilled right through them. These holes have a function in folk-magic and spiritual development, being used for the promotion of fertility, healing and seership. Some holed stones are pilgrims' stations visited during saints' Patterns. Each has its own particular custom associated with it, such as looking

Inscribed pillar-stones.
Left: broken pillar with floreated cross and remains of wheel-cross, Kilmakedar, County Kerry, Ireland;
Centre: Gallarus, County Kerry, Ireland, with wheel-cross;
Right: Llandilo, Dyfed, Wales, with ogham inscription and Coptic-type cross.

through the hole, passing something, or holding hands through it. There is a hole in the top of an ogham-inscribed pillar-stone that stands at a stopping-place on the Saint's Road at Kilmakedar on the Dingle Peninsula. At Glencolmkille, a stone slab marking the stopping-place called Farranmacbride has a hole at the centre of the wheel-cross near the top. It is said that the pilgrim who looks through the hole while 'doing the round' will get a glimpse of heaven.

Holes have a function in folk-magic and spiritual development, being used for the promotion of fertility, healing and seership.

The Pictish cross-slab at Aberlemno has one of the four round corners of the cross drilled right through, and many wheel-headed crosses have not one hole, but four, that connect the front with the back. More generally, the whole genre of 'four-holed' and wheel-headed crosses are instances of the veneration of holy holed stones. The motif of the four holes, present already in German Celtic stones from the sixth century BCE, appears also in the early pillar-cross from Carn Caca at Melin-cwrt, Resolfen, in West Glamorgan. This has a carved circle in which is a cross potent. This kind of cross is composed of four T-shaped pieces, which alludes to the *tau* cross, symbol of the father of monasticism, St Anthony of Egypt. In the four angles of this cross are four depressions or dots that appear in later crosses as holes or circles.

Some of these standing cross-stones are likely to have been holy stones sacred to the elder faith that were reconsecrated as Christian monuments by being carved with the symbols of the newer religion. 'The earliest preachers of Christianity do not seem to have made violent attacks upon the creeds and beliefs of their converts,' wrote Alfred Rimmer in *Ancient Stone Crosses of England* (Virtue and Co, 1875), '... they pointed to the groves and holy wells, and dedicated them in another name. Crossroads also were held peculiarly sacred in the early times, and even as far back as the period of the Druids they were marked by upright stones, not dissimilar to those we see at Stonehenge, though, of course, much smaller, and these stones were chiselled on the upper part with a cross in relief.' Although many Celtic churches were founded on new sites, some took over places of Pagan sanctity. The standing stones that marked the old sanctuaries were re-used in the fabric of the new building, or allowed to remain in the churchyard re-consecrated as crosses. There are many instances of this process throughout the Celtic realms. In Scotland, the Fifeshire church of Dunino incorporates megaliths which were Christianized with crosses inscribed upon them. An example of a standing stone that became a kind of cross can be seen in the churchyard at Bridell in Dyfed, which contains a megalith upon which is an ogham inscription commemorating 'Nettasagrus, descendant of Brecos'. A cross inscribed inside a circle was added later. In Wales, the re-use of ancient stones was a common practice throughout history, continuing well into the nineteenth century. In 1876, for instance, an ogham-inscribed wheel-cross slab at Staynton in Pembrokeshire was re-used as the tombstone of T. Harries, who died on 30 January that year, aged 84.

RE-CONSECRATED STONES

Re-dedication of megaliths by churchmen is recorded in ancient accounts of the acts of early Celtic priests and monks. Brittany contains many standing stones that have been made into Christian monuments by having a cross carved upon them. There are probably more in that region than anywhere else in western Europe; but it was commonplace throughout the Celtic realms. In his 'The Acts of Patrick' in *The Book of Armagh*, Tirechan describes how St Patrick carved a cross on a rock at Lia na Manach near the church of Kilmore in County Mayo. The Welsh saint, Samson, seems to have been one of the most active re-dedicators. The 'Life of St Samson' (*The Lives of the British Saints*, Honourable Society of Cymmrodorion, 1908) recounts that when the early sixth-century saint was passing through Cornwall on his way from Wales to Brittany he travelled through a region called Tricurius. There he encountered some people performing ceremonies at what the chronicler calls an 'abominable image', that is, a standing stone. Unlike his Biblical namesake, who toppled the pillars of the Philistines, this Samson did not fell the stone, but re-dedicated it to

Re-dedication of megaliths by churchmen is recorded in ancient accounts of the acts of early Celtic priests and monks.

Christian use by cutting a cross upon it. Although the exact place that this occurred is not identified, there are several possible locations.

In Glamorgan, south Wales, are the standing stones called *Ffust Samson* (Samson's flail), Samson's Jack and *Carreg Samson* (Samson's stone). Elsewhere in Wales are other stones called *Carreg Samson*. The name is given to a standing stone on the mountainside at Llandewi

Brefi, a stone cross near the church porch at Llanbadarn Fawr near Aberystwyth, and two cromlechs in north Pembrokeshire, Dyfed. Also in this area are stones called *Marbl Samson* (Samson's marble) and *Bys Samson* (Samson's finger). Samson's stones in south Wales stand on the route of his journey from Llantwit Major to Dôl in Brittany, and, not surprisingly, there are St Samson's stones in Brittany, too. A menhir at Mont-Dôl, Ile-et-Vilaine, is called St Samson's Mitre, and at Penvern, Côte-du-Nord, is another menhir named after the saint. Next to it stands a chapel dedicated to Samson, which was constructed between 1575 and 1631.

In Wales, the megalith sacred to another early Celtic missionary, St Beuno, still stands at Berriew in Powys, in the shape of Beuno's Stone. The animal-related rites conducted until the last century at Beuno's shrine, at Clynnog Fawr in the Lleyn, were the direct continuation of Celtic Paganism. It seems that, like many priests of the Celtic church, Beuno took over the shrines of the elder faith for Christian use while altering their ceremonial character very little. Elsewhere, other Celtic priests, whose names are not recorded, also appropriated the holy stones of the elder faith. At Llanfaelog in Anglesey, a prehistoric cup-marked menhir was re-dedicated by having a cross cut upon it, while at East Worlington in Devon is the megalith called the Long Stone, which bears no fewer than five incised crosses.

Some Cornish antiquaries have considered a number of the more archaic-looking stone crosses in that county to be of druidic, rather than Christian origin. In their form, they appear close to continental stones of the Hallstatt period, such as the Kilchberg stone in south Germany. Thus it is possible that at least some of the Cornish crosses are stones of the elder faith, re-consecrated for Christian use. 'The early pillar "crosses", though accounted Christian when tested by inscription and decoration,' wrote Walter Johnson in 1912 in his *Byways in Archaeology*, 'may yet have an earlier origin ... many of the crosses and calvaries of Brittany, "with shapeless sculpture decked", are merely primitive menhirs adapted by the Christian artificer, and anyone who, like the writer, has had the opportunity of comparing the Breton sites with the kindred group of our English Brittany, will readily agree that a similar story may be told of Cornwall.'

Although it ceased in the early middle ages in Britain, when people began to destroy standing stones, the alteration of megaliths into Christian monuments continued in France until shortly before the Revolution. A re-dedicated menhir at Dôl (Ile-et-Vilaine), bears a

metal cross on top of the 9.5 m-tall (30 ft) stone, while the Dolmen de la Belle Vue at Carnac has a stone cross set upon it. In 1826, Sir Richard Colt Hoare published an engraving of this cross under the title of 'Triumph of Christianity over Druidism'. The process of converting megaliths into crosses was associated usually with some specific local religious activity. For instance, in 1674, in connection with the construction of a new chapel nearby, a prehistoric megalith at Penvern in Brittany was re-dedicated by a Christian priest. This involved cutting down its summit to make a cross, and carving Christian emblems upon the remaining body of the stone. At Rungleo in Finistère is the Croix des Douze Apôtres. This is another megalith upon which Christian figures have been carved. At Pleumeur-Bodou in the Côtes-du-Nord is one which in the eighteenth century was cut with the cross and symbols of Christ's passion.

The last-known conversion of a megalith in France occurred in Alsace in 1787, when a megalith near Althorn known as the

> *The last-known conversion of a megalith in France occurred in Alsace in 1787, when a megalith near Althorn known as the Breitenstein was re-carved as the 'Twelve Apostles Stone'.*

Breitenstein was re-carved as the result of a fulfilled vow. Thus, the Breitenstein became another 'Twelve Apostles Stone'. Not all Celtic Crosses in France are altered megaliths, however. Ancient crosses similar to those in Cornwall and the Isles of Scilly exist in several Breton churchyards. The crosses are of both the wheel-head and plain form. The churchyard at Ploudalmezou has a notable wheel-head cross on a stepped base. It is dedicated to St Pol de Léon, as are the other crosses there. The holy well of Saint-Cado is topped by a fine Celtic cross with a crucifixion at the centre reminiscent of that on the Cross of the Scriptures at Clonmacnois.

OPPOSITE: The 'Twelve Apostles Stone' (Breitenstein) near Althorn, Alsace, France, a megalith re-carved as a Christian cross in 1787. *(Nigel Pennick)*

7

THE EVOLUTION OF THE CELTIC CROSS

At the end of the fourth century, the mission of St Ninian to the
people who lived north of the Roman province of Britain led
to the foundation of the first Christian church in Caledonia.
This was the so-called *Candida Casa* (White House) at Whithorn in
Galloway. In the fifth and sixth centuries, the *Candida Casa* was a
centre of Christian missionary activity in northern Britain and Ireland.
St Enda, founder of the early monastery at Killeany on the Aran island
of Inishmore, was an alumnus of Whithorn. There are few remains
of Ninian's church, but a number of early Christian tomb-slabs at
Whithorn and Kirkmadrine. The oldest Christian monument known
from Scotland was discovered close to the site of Ninian's *Candida
Casa*. It is an early fifth-century stone carved with a Latin inscription
commemorating Latinus, his daughter and his grandson, Barrovadus,
who set up the monument. At Kirkmadrine are three more memorial
stones with Latin inscriptions and the *chi-rho* monogram. The associated
holy place of Physgyll, St Ninian's Cave, on the foreshore about 5 km
(3 miles) from Whithorn, has a number of early memorial crosses, some
carved in the living rock, and some on separate stones.

MEMORIALS AND CROSS-SLABS

Most Welsh memorial stones dating from the fifth to the seventh
century are megaliths, unworked stones whose natural shapes were
appropriate for inscriptions to be carved on them with the minimum
of effort. Like the earlier megaliths, they were intended to stand upright as memorials that marked the burial places of important people,
or sometimes the boundaries between territories. The earliest inscriptions are in Roman capitals, recalling that it was only a few years since

Varieties of crosses and stones at the meeting-point of Paganism and Christianity, using motifs derived from *Irminsul*.
Top row: Osmondwall Chapel, Walls and Flotta Parish, Orkney; St Nicholas Chapel, Papa Stronsay, Orkney.
Below: cross with runes from Ballaugh, Isle of Man; stone with 'Pagan Cross', Dover, England.
Right: Danish runestone with *Irminsul* pattern containing runes.

Britain was a province of the Roman Empire. Later, however, as the memory of being Roman faded, this changed, and half-uncials, a character-type taken from Christian manuscripts, were used instead.

It appears to have been customary among the Pagan Anglo-Saxons who did not cremate their dead to bury a runestone with the body. Around the seventh century, stonecarvers began to incise crosses upon similar stones, some of which were intended to lie flat above the dead person, and not to stand up as a tombstone. Northumbrian 'pillow-stones' are known from the monastic cemeteries of Hartlepool and Lindisfarne, and a few other places including Billingham and Birtley in County Durham. Their name is misleading, for they were not placed beneath the head of the corpse, but over the face or on the chest.

73

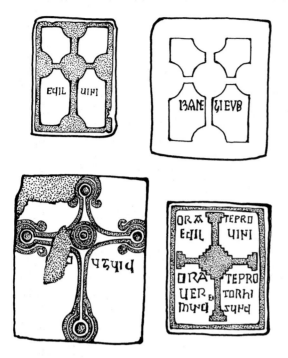

Seventh- or eighth-century Northumbrian 'pillow-stones' from the Anglian nunnery at Hartlepool, Cleveland, England.
Dedications, clockwise from top left: Ediluni; Hanegneub; Uermund and Torhtsuid; --uguid.

Closely related to Irish slabs, of which the largest collection can be seen at Clonmacnois, the Northumbrian pillow-stones are rectangular, with an incised cross-pattern. In Merovingian France at this time, it was becoming fashionable to mark Christian burials by flat slabs carved with ring-crosses.

Related to the Celtic wheel-head is the type of flat slab which has a cross at each end. These end-crosses are connected by a bar that forms another cross at the centre dividing the field into four panels, inside which is ornament. Early examples of this type exist at Sockburn in County Durham and Spennithorne in North Yorkshire. The majority of known slabs of this kind (about 40 in all) are in East Anglia in the region of Cambridge, Peterborough and Norwich, and made of Barnack stone. The most numerous find of these cross-slabs was made in 1811 beneath the earthworks of Cambridge Castle, which was built by the Normans around the year 1070 on the graveyard of an Anglo-Saxon monastery. A similar slab, illustrated here, exists at Peterborough Cathedral, and comparable stones without interlace patterns are known from Sussex at Chithurst, Steyning and Stedham.

Many ancient churches and abbeys contain ancient crosses and cross-slabs. Their state of preservation and the conditions under which they are kept varies greatly. More often than not, they seem merely to be

OPPOSITE: Cross-slabs.
Top row, left to right:
Sinniness; Drummore; Craignarget (all in Dumfries and Galloway, Scotland).
Centre row: Lawrence's Church, Papil, West Burra, Shetland; Llangeinwen, Anglesey, Wales; Peterborough Cathedral, Cambridgeshire, England; Bakewell, Derbyshire, England.
Horizontal stones:
(upper) Cambridge Castle, Cambridgeshire; (lower) Hansted, Aarhus, Denmark.

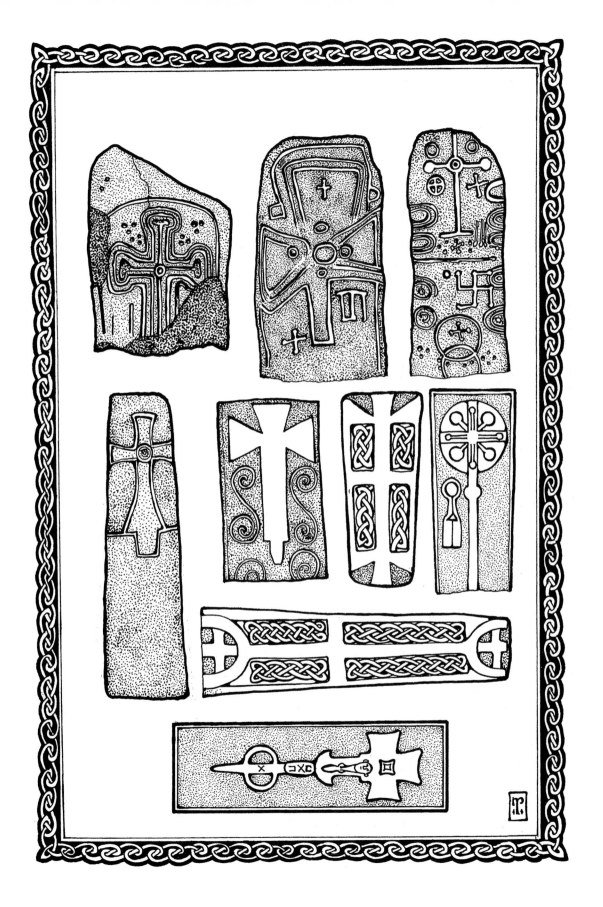

an inconvenience for the church authorities, so they are relegated to dusty corners inside the building, or languish outside in stone-heaps behind chicken wire amid gardening tools and refuse. The historical significance of the stones seems not to affect the way they are handled: even the monuments of kings are treated in this manner. Perhaps the

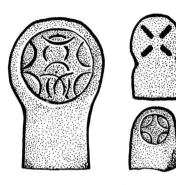

Pre-conquest English tombstones:
Top to bottom: Adel, with patterns derived from solar phenomena; Bakewell Church, Derbyshire; Broadway, Hereford and Worcester; Bakewell.

least threatened are those stones actually built into the fabric, like the pieces of Celtic Cross in the walls of many churches, such as Little St Mary's in Cambridge and Llangeinwen in Anglesey. Such stones as these are visible, but it is clear that there are many more ancient carved stones embedded invisibly in the fabric of churches, castles, bridges and sea walls. Numerous fine examples came to light at Bakewell in Derbyshire in 1841, when the tower and transepts of the church were demolished during reconstruction. Sculptured stones removed from the old building included around 300 ancient monuments, ranging in date from before the Norman conquest to the thirteenth century. Seventy of them were retained, and built into the south porch of the church, but the rest were re-used and buried in the new walls, without being recorded in any way. Thus, a remarkable opportunity was lost, for many of those still visible show the many variant forms that the wheel-cross took. With the present decline of religion, however, many ancient churches are likely to be demolished in the near future, and doubtless more fascinating ancient stones will emerge again, if we who are interested in our heritage remain alert to developments.

PICTISH STONES AND CROSSES

Before the immigration of the Scots from Ireland, the Picts of northern Britain possessed their own style of Celtic art. Although the Picts probably produced wonderful textiles, leatherwork, woodwork and metalwork, little has survived, and it is almost entirely through memorial stones that their art is known. J. Romilly Allen, who made an intensive study of Pictish memorial stones (*The Early Christian Monuments of Scotland*, The Pinkfoot Press, 1993) classified them into three categories. His Class I stones, which may date from the seventh century, are natural, largely unworked, megaliths upon which various emblems or 'symbols' were carved. As the meaning or symbolism of these emblems is unknown, it is rather paradoxical that the name usually given to the stones on which they appear is 'symbol stones'. However, by drawing parallels with the customs of tattooing warriors in other cultures, it may be surmised that the tattoos worn by the Picts were in the form of such 'symbols', made in honour of the gods. As in many warrior societies, it is likely that each Pictish warrior was known by his unique personal array of tattoos, which were reproduced on his memorial stone when he died.

Around the middle of the eighth century, Pictish stonecarvers began to use the cross in their designs, and Biblical images began to enter their repertoire of images. Romilly Allen's definition of these Class II Pictish stones categorizes them as: 'erect cross-slabs or recumbent coped stones with symbols [sic] and Celtic ornament sculptured in relief.' Although the cross is a significant part of the design of these stones, there are no known representations of the crucifixion or indeed of any images that can be interpreted as representing episodes from the New Testament. These are the monuments that were set up after the acceptance of Northumbrian Catholicism in the year 710 by the Pictish high king Nechtan IV mac Derile.

The Class II slabs have crosses whose form and content is related to contemporary known manuscripts and probably also tapestries, now lost. Fourteen variants of cross have been identified, the most common of which have rounded indentations at the crossing in the manner of the four-holed crosses. Equally prevalent is the rectilinear cross composed of squares, with squares at the crossing. Similar varieties were made in Ireland. There are fine examples on stones at Clonmacnois, Durrow and elsewhere. Among the earliest in this style are the Pictish stones from Aberlemno churchyard, Birsay, Meigle, Papil, Rossie Priory and St Vigeans. All have sculpture in relatively low relief, including Pictish emblems of the Pagan period, perhaps

As in many warrior societies, it is likely that each Pictish warrior was known by his unique personal array of tattoos, which were reproduced on his memorial stone when he died.

reproducing the tattoos of the dead. Development of the style led, around the year 800, to more complex work. The Hilton of Cadboll stone in Easter Ross is a good example. It is carved with scenes from Biblical mythology, hunting figures and Pictish emblems. The whole emblematical scheme of these stones is syncretic, with elements from many sources. Certain elements come from indigenous Pictish Paganism. The Biblical figures may have been influenced by Mercian art, while the monsters and demons have similarities with those described in the early illustrated text, *The Marvels of the East*, which was current in Northumbrian monasteries at the time.

At Rossie Priory, in Tayside, is a stone sometimes called a 'page in stone'. Frequently, the design of this stone is assumed to be a sculptural representation of a page of a book. Equally, however, it could represent one of the woven textile banners that were used by travelling priests in conjunction with portable altars. There are parallels, too, with the Pagan memorial stones of Gotland. The whole stone has an interlace border which merges with the three free arms of the cross at the left, right and top. The centre of the cross is a circle with key-patterns in the middle, while the cross-shaft bears carvings of horseriders. In the panels surrounding the cross are depictions of various things: an angel, or fury; a human figure holding the necks of two birds in the manner of ancient images of the goddess Artemis, Lady of the Beasts; a hound, horsemen and other animals. There are only a few Pictish stones of this type that show the typical Pictish images on the front of the cross-slab. At this period, it was more usual to carve them on the rear of the slab. Possibly, converted Picts who still wore the old Pagan tattoos, or still honoured them as ancestral heraldry, were commemorated thus. The typically 'Pictish' images on this slab are a crescent-and-rod and the enigmatic stylized beast variously described as a hippogriff, elephant, seahorse or walrus.

In the churchyard at Aberlemno in Tayside is one of the most famous Pictish cross-slabs, which amalgamates the slab-form with the wheel-headed Celtic Cross. The slab is sculptured so that the cross-form stands out strongly from the background. The upright panel that would be the shaft if the cross were free-standing is carved with a complex interlace pattern based on three circles. This 'supports' the lower part of the wheel-cross, which is carved as though it were separate, being distinguished by a more open, separate interlace pattern. The cross-arms on either side of the centre bear key-patterns, while the centre is composed of six spirals around a seventh, central, one. The cross is topped with an X-formed interlace. One of the four 'holes' in the cross has been drilled right through, making it a holed stone. This hole destroys part of the carving on the back, showing it to be a later, vernacular, addition for magical purposes. The supporting slab is carved with spiralling animal-ornament, and the cross's top is flanked by two stylized beasts. Other notable Pictish cross-slabs of this style include those from Glamis, carved with fine interlace and beasts, at Scoonie and at Meigle.

Later in the ninth century, the so-called 'boss style' was developed. This is characterized by an adventurous departure in design employing large round bosses sculpted with interlace, which are sometimes

Pictish cross-slab from Aberlemno, Tayside, Scotland. The top right depression has been drilled through to make the cross into a holed stone. The spiral centre is reminiscent of the main emblems on the Gotland memorial stones.

accompanied by serpents. These serpentine bosses may be a representation of the magical druidic 'serpents' eggs' or 'adder stones' mentioned by Pliny in his *Natural History*: 'In the summer, numerous snakes entwine themselves in a ball, held together by a secretion from their bodies and by spittle ... the druids value it highly. It is said to ensure success in lawsuits and a favourable reception with princes.' Whatever the meaning of bosses, the style was used on slabs in the Isle of Man and free-standing crosses in western Scotland, Iona and Ireland. Among the notable examples of Pictish stones in the 'boss style' are the Roadside Cross at Aberlemno, the cross from Nigg in Easter Ross in Highland Region, another at Shandwick nearby, and the Pictish shrine at St Andrews. The Nigg stone has remarkably fine carvings, and bosses composed variously of knotwork of serpentine and rectilinear form, and spirals. This highly elaborate, sophisticated and doubtless very expensive style was not maintained for long. Soon, stonemasons adopted more simplified designs, examples of which can be seen in the stones from Fowlis Wester, Tayside and Rosemarkie in the Highland Region.

A Pictish stone from Dunfallandy in Tayside has a cross based upon squares, but with rounded forms at the angles of the cross. These rounded forms appear at the top of the shaft beneath the cross-head, which is in more prominent relief than the rest of the carvings. Each of the four arms of the cross-head is sculpted with prominent bosses, five each on the upright parts and three each on the cross-arms. Panels of spiralwork form the background to the bosses, while the whole slab is bordered by interlacework in the manner of the Gotland stones. Between the border and the cross are ten panels bearing beasts and angels. The back of the slab is purely pictorial, with horsemen, dogs, a centaur with twin axes, beasts and a man who stands between four animals, often interpreted as representing Daniel among the lions.

The stones later classified as Pictish Class III came into being in the late ninth century after the unification of Pictland and Dalriada by King Kenneth mac Alpin. These Class III stones are in the form of free-standing crosses and cross-slabs. They differ from the earlier slabs because the Pictish emblems are absent. Perhaps, because by now they considered themselves to be wholly Christian, those commemorated by the stones no longer bore their identifying

The richly sculptured Pictish 'boss-style' cross-slab from Nigg, Easter Ross, Highland Region, Scotland, broken by religious zealots and later re-assembled. *(Historic Scotland)*

tattoos or honoured the old heraldry of their ancestors. Also, because they are slabs, these stones differ from the contemporary free-standing wheel-headed crosses of the Celtic church. It is likely that when King Nechtan IV mac Derile adopted Catholic Christianity from the Anglians of Northumbria and expelled the Celtic priesthood from Pictland, it was considered to be politically expedient not to use the Celtic Cross, which had clear Irish origins. Instead, the Pictish masons developed a national style that served as an emblem of their religious allegiance to Rome rather than Ireland.

The Pictish masons developed a national style that served as an emblem of their religious allegiance to Rome rather than Ireland.

As a national style, it was maintained long after Dalriada and Pictland became Scotland.

At Dupplin, west of Perth, Anglian influence is apparent in the sculptures of vinescrolls and beasts. There is similar ornament on the cross at Crieff in Tayside. Mustachioed men resembling those on Muiredach's Cross at Monasterboice are on the Dupplin cross, and on a cross-slab at Benvie, Tayside. They may represent Scots rather than Picts, who were shown bearded. A cross-slab from Inchbrayock, Tayside, has a squared cross on one side, accompanied by figures, interlace and a beast. The rear, as with so many Pictish stones, has human figures engaged in hunting and Biblical scenes. The interlace and spirals on the Inchbrayock stone, like much Pictish carving of this period, is a free and dynamic interpretation of the underlying geometrical matrix.

There are few known Pictish stones that are carved with the crucified Christ. A cross-shaft from Monifieth near Dundee has a crucifixion, but on a stone influenced by Anglo-Danish tradition. It is possible that before the unification of the Picts and Scots there were no such representations. It is equally possible, however, that early Pictish depictions of the crucifixion have all been destroyed, for many stones were damaged or smashed in the suppression of Catholic worship in the sixteenth century. An idea of what happened can be seen on a Pictish cross-slab from Woodwray on Tayside which has had the cross carefully chipped away, leaving only its surrounding beasts and border. So it is not unlikely that Protestant zealots, in attempting to extirpate what they considered to be idolatry, destroyed all of the Pictish stones that bore images of the crucifixion, giving us a false impression of the actual practices of the Pictish masons.

8
FORM AND PATTERN
IN CELTIC ART

Structurally, Celtic art is based upon a hidden, but ever-present geometric basis. Sacred geometry has been practised in the British Isles since the time of the megalith builders. When building in dressed stone was introduced from Roman-influenced lands, a complementary sacred geometry, originating ultimately in ancient Egypt, was added to the indigenous tradition. Knowledge of sacred geometry was part of the trade secrets of the mason, and couched in esoteric terms impenetrable to the layperson. Plutarch stated that the Egyptian priests and priestesses carried three sacred rods, dedicated respectively to Isis, Osiris and Horus. The rod of Isis represented origination, and was coloured black. The rod of Osiris signified the receptive principle, being coloured red. Horus's rod was blue, symbolizing the result of combination. They were ascribed the numbers 5, 4 and 3. When they were brought together, a right-angled triangle was formed.

This is the basis of the 47th proposition of Euclid, the geometrical theorem associated with Pythagoras, which proves how any triangle the sides of which measure 3, 4 and 5 units contains a right angle. Although it may seem deceptively simple, it was not common knowledge in earlier times, being a closely guarded secret of initiates of the mystery schools. Nevertheless it is the fundamental basis of all geometry. In medieval Britain, this mystery was embodied in the device known as the Druids' Cord or *snor*, a rope with 12 knots dividing it into 13 equal sections which was used in land measure and building to lay out right angles on the ground. The *snor* and mystic rod can be seen in old illustrations of master masons from the middle ages, and Sir Christopher Wren's ceremonial measuring rod is preserved in St Paul's Cathedral in London. He used it in the foundation and completion ceremonies of the great sacred building.

GEOMETRY AND SYMBOLISM

Laying out anything by geometry is a symbolic re-creation of the world. Because of this, ancient traditions portray the creator as the supreme geometer of the universe. In the fourth century BCE, Plato stated that Zeus is the supreme geometer, and the Greek legend of how Apollo determined the location of the *omphalos* at Delphi employs a form of landscape geometry. Medieval illustrations of the creation show God the Father as the grand geometrician of the universe, compasses in hand, measuring out the sacred geometry of the cosmos. This transcendent image was expressed beautifully by John Milton in his *Paradise Lost*, written in the mid-seventeenth century:

> Then stayed the fervid wheels, and in his hand
> He took the golden compasses, prepared
> In God's eternal store, to circumscribe
> This Universe, and all created things.
> One foot he centred, and the other turned
> Round through the vast profundity obscure,
> And said, 'Thus far extend, thus far thy bounds,
> Be this thy just circumference, O world!'

This image was popularized by the druidic mystic William Blake in his engraving *The Ancient of Days*.

In ancient Europe, the divine order of the cosmos was represented geometrically by the pattern of the rectilinear grid. The grid is a powerful symbol of the underlying structure of existence, and of divine or human dominion over it. Signifying the works of the great architect of the universe, in the shape of law and order, authority and justice, the rectilinear grid is present in Celtic art. It served to depict holy figures in both the Pagan and Christian traditions. The back of an image of the horned god Cernunnos from Roqueperteuse in southern France has a grid in the form of four squares within another square. Repeating cross-patterns based on the grid were being carved on Celtic stones 600 years before the Christian religion came into being. Tesselations of T-shapes with crosses can be seen in Germany on Celtic memorials dating from the La Tène period. The lower piece of a stone image in human form, found at Steinenbronn in Baden-Württemberg and now kept in the Württembergisches Landesmuseum in Stuttgart, is carved with designs that were used again on Christian artefacts in the British Isles. A thousand years later, an evangelist in the *Book of Durrow* wears a cloak with a grid pattern upon it.

Played on a gridded board, the Celtic game known as *Tawlbwrdd* in Wales, and *Fidcheall* or *Brannumh* in Ireland, was more than just a pastime, for it symbolized the land and the royal order necessary for its proper functioning according to divine laws. Because of this, one of the official emblems of the judge in ancient Wales was a *Tawlbwrdd* board. As the ruling principle, the rectilinear grid underlies Celtic artwork on stone crosses and manuscripts. Just as good laws and just administration of a land should be apparent only through the proper functioning of society, so the guiding grid of Celtic art is usually just an underlying principle invisible in the finished artwork.

The men who made the Celtic high crosses were the best stonemasons of their day. Their craft is evident both in the actual construction of the high crosses from several pieces of stone, fitted together in a masterly manner; and in the use of geometry in their design. Their Celtic understanding of geometry was masterful, evident in the interlace and spiral designs not only of stone crosses but also of illuminated manuscripts, metalwork and stonecarving. Here, the Christian tradition did not extirpate the earlier Pagan vision, but continued and developed it. The geometric grid that underlies a considerable amount of surviving ornament on Celtic Crosses is of one or other of two basic forms, the square or diamond. The construction of both patterns was one of the fundamental mysteries of ancient geometry. The construction of the square grid is self-evident, but the diamond pattern is more esoteric. This pattern, which has what the Celtic art researcher George Bain (*The Methods of Construction*, McLellan, 1951) called the 'Pictish Proportion' of 1:¾, is better known in the craft of masonry as the Egyptian Diamond. It is a lozenge-shaped figure composed of four 3-4-5 triangles, so that it measures eight units in length and six units wide, with a perimeter of 20 units and an area of 24 square units. Thus, the Egyptian mystery of the three holy rods of Isis, Osiris and Horus is embodied in Celtic art.

The crucifixion scene at the centre of the high cross of Muiredach at Monasterboice, Ireland. *(Nigel Pennick)*

When the crossmakers used key-patterns or circles and spirals, these, too, were based on underlying grids. These methods were used in mainland Europe before the Celts entered the British Isles, as attested by examples from southern France and Germany, such as the Steinenbronn image. The Egyptian Diamond itself appears on the cross at Moone. The underlying geometry of figures, too, is shown overtly in a few instances, for example on Muiredach's Cross at Monasterboice in a panel that shows a staff-holding man between two swordsmen. One of them is pulling open the middle figure's garments in the shape of an Egyptian Diamond, to point his sword at the man's navel, while the figure made by the victim's staff and other assailant's sword is the 3-4-5 triangle. Several other martial arts designs on Irish crosses express their underlying sacred geometry through the position of weapons.

According to ancient British Bardic teachings, beneath the outer, visible form of matter lies a subtle matrix upon which all things are based. The old Welsh word *manred* denotes this invisible matrix of existence; the atoms and molecules, the structures and geometrical relationships that make up physical reality. These patterns are not eternally fixed, but flow through time, expressing its essence through an almost infinite variety of forms. More than any other art form, Celtic art displays these ever-changing dynamic patterns of *manred*. Like nature, the geometric matrices upon which Celtic tesselations, spirals and knotwork are based are continuous. In their plurality, all of the different pattern-styles are infinitely interchangeable. They can easily fade into one another imperceptibly. The patterns of *manred* are infinitely changing, but they are not meaningless. Thus, esoterically, the patterns of Celtic art are the fixed artistic representations of the ever-flowing particles of *manred*, for all is flux.

According to ancient British Bardic teachings, beneath the outer, visible form of matter lies a subtle matrix upon which all things are based.

Celtic artists use the principle of self-similarity in conjunction with the underlying geometry of Celtic art. This is where a form at one size is included within a similar form on a larger scale. This principle, recognized in Europe over 3,000 years ago by the people of the Hallstatt culture, was re-affirmed by Benoit Mandelbrot in 1980 when he discovered fractal mathematics. Self-similarity is the innate quality of an integral structure that manifests itself as repeating patterns from the smallest level to the largest. Thus, the smallest part of existence, the

Opposite: Varieties of
pattern on Celtic Crosses.
Top row, left to right: panel
from cross at Llantwit
Major, South Glamorgan,
Wales; Muiredach's Cross,
Monasterboice, Louth,
Ireland; Littleton Drew,
Wiltshire, England.
Second row: Llantwit Major;
Nevern, Dyfed; Bath
Abbey, Bath, Avon,
England.
Third row: Monasterboice.
Fourth row: Inchbrayock,
Tayside, Scotland; St Just-
in-Penwith, Cornwall;
(above) Maughold, Isle of
Man; *(below)* Mawgan-in-
Pyder, Cornwall.

microcosm, is linked to the largest, the macrocosm. This link is not a crude reflection, but a more subtle, ordered repetition through the middle ground that lies between the small and the large. Self-similarity means that a structure that is present at one level is repeated on both higher and lower levels. Thus, the overall pattern of a Celtic artefact may be repeated again in the details of the ornament upon it. Just as there is no place for a void middle ground in nature, so in Celtic art there are no empty spaces, just as there are no blank spaces in the cosmos. Structure is present at every point, with each small part simultaneously reflecting the essential structure of the whole. Thus, all is inseparable. This essential oneness has been the guiding principle of Celtic art from its emergence 2,700 years ago until the present day. It is the *leitmotif* of the Celtic Cross.

Self-similarity is apparent throughout Celtic art. The magnificent bull-headed torc found at Trichtingen in Germany is a fine example of how the principle of self-similarity operates. Each of the bull-head terminals on the torc wears a torc around its neck, the terminals of which are torcs, and so on. In Christian Ireland, the same principle was observed in the construction of shrines which were contained in identical, but larger, sacred containers, which themselves were kept in churches of the same form. In turn, the churches were designed symbolically to be images of the body of Christ and also the form of God's creation, the cosmos.

ICONIC AND ANICONIC ART

Although in the West we are used to images, the art of the sacred need not be composed of pictures that portray any specific aspect of the visible world. The division between those who believe that the sacred can be portrayed through images and those who claim it cannot lies at the root of the two opposing theories of sacred art: the iconic, which portrays images of the divine; and the aniconic, which suggests the presence of the divine through non-figurative motifs. Aniconic art lends itself more readily to contemplation than does figurative depiction. Aniconic elements reflect the structure of the unseen rather than the outer world of things, while representational art depicts the outer appearance of real things and the imaginary appearance of transcendent things. Aniconic art allows the viewer to behold a deeper reality than ever can an image. This kind of art should not be considered abstract, however, for it is based upon the transcendent principles of *manred*, while abstraction is often without any spiritual content whatsoever. The aniconic allows us to contemplate the realities that lie beyond the visible world of image; by not objectivizing the unseen, it avoids the possibility of devaluing or trivializing spiritual elements while allowing human beings to enter the world of the unseen. It prevents the inner ideal from being distorted into an external object of worship, thereby ensuring that nothing comes between the human being and the unseen realm of the divine.

It is clear that aniconism was the guiding principle of ancient Celtic Paganism. In the fourth century BCE, the Celtic general Brennos captured the Greek shrine of Delphi. According to Diodorus Siculus: 'When he encountered only images of stone and wood, he laughed at them, to think that men, believing that the gods had human form, should erect their images in wood and stone.' Only later, under Roman influence, did the Celts portray their goddesses and gods in human form. According to medieval Welsh bardic writings, the ancient British sages taught that even the name of the Absolute should never be spoken. They held that it is blasphemous to utter the name of God, and also unnecessary, because the whole world is already a manifestation of the divine. This idea was current among many people in the British Isles until quite recently. In 1690, the East Anglian philosopher Sir Thomas Browne wrote in his *Christian Morals*: 'To thoughtful observators the whole world is a phylactery, and every thing we see is an item of the wisdom, power and goodness of God.' Around the same period, the Welsh Bards stated: 'It is considered presumptuous to utter this name in the hearing of any man in the world. Nevertheless, every thing calls him inwardly by this name – the sea and land, earth and air, all the visibles and invisibles of the world, whether on the earth or in the sky – all the worlds of all the celestials and the terrestrials – every intellectual being and existence ....' Similarly, it is likely that the early Celtic Christians believed that to depict God literally in an image was as unnecessary as it was blasphemous.

Charges that those who make images are practising image worship – idolatry – were made first by Jews and Muslims against Pagans and Christians and later by Protestant Christians against Catholic members of the same religion. The principle of aniconism is best known as the underlying principle of Judaic and Islamic law, but has sometimes been present in Christianity as well. Most notably, aniconism was enforced in the religious art of the Orthodox Eastern Empire during the iconoclastic period (730–843), when religious images were destroyed in the pursuit of piety. Even in the West at this time, iconoclasm was admired, when Bishop Claudius of Turin ordered crosses to be destroyed as idolatrous, and forbade all pilgrimages to the shrines of saints. In Christianity, however, unlike in Islam, aniconism did not last.

It is likely that the early Celtic Christians believed that to depict God literally in an image was as unnecessary as it was blasphemous.

After a period of violent conflict between those who wanted images and those who opposed them, an ecumenical council of the Eastern Orthodox Church finally decided to end iconoclasm, and reasserted the use of images in sacred art. 'God himself is outside all possible description or representation,' asserted the council's priests, 'but since the divine word took human nature upon itself, which it reintegrated into its original form by infusing it with divine beauty, God can and must be venerated through the human image of Christ.' This declaration was made in the form of a prayer to Our Lady, for it was through her that the divine form took upon human substance, bringing it from the otherworld into the realm of the human senses.

Although Dungal of Pavia, an Irish monk living in Italy, was one of the objectors to the iconoclasm of Bishop Claudius, it appears that the Celtic church was affected by iconoclasm. Celtic art has always had a strong non-figurative element, and often Celtic artists preferred to continue their pre-Christian love for symbolic patterns rather than making any realistic representation of divine beings. Thus the symbolic forms of crosses were erected in preference to the literalistic representations of Christ's crucifixion. Later, even when the material world was represented, it was in a stylized form, avoiding naturalism. The zoomorphic interlace and plant-forms of Celtic Crosses are so highly stylized that they cannot be mistaken for the real thing. This stylization helps to prevent the worshipper from concentrating on nothing but particulars, thereby remaining unaware of the deep roots of all being.

CRAFT TECHNIQUES
AND CELTIC ORNAMENT

Many researchers into Celtic Crosses have emphasized the close relationship between the designs used on ornamental metalwork and stone sculpture. It is evident that small items of metalwork, whether sacred objects, ornaments, jewellery or weapons, were easily transported from place to place and thus could serve as models for craftspeople in localities distant from their places of origin. Thus, new artistic styles could be disseminated as small objects. However, we should remember that while much metalwork has survived from the first millennium the undoubtedly more common wooden, bone, ivory, textile and leather items were not as durable and have decayed. Only a few have been preserved until the present day. So when we look at metalwork, we are seeing only one part of the repertoire of Celtic craftspeople.

Christian elements of design may have been disseminated into Celtic art before the religious beliefs to which they refer. When Christian elements such as the *chi-rho*, cross and fish appear in metalwork or other art of this conversion period, it is not a certain sign that the makers or owners were members of the religion. Today in everyday life we can see people wearing crosses and crucifixes as lucky charms, along with ankhs, yang-and-yin signs, Stars of David, pentagrams and Hammers of Thor, among other sacred amulets. Perhaps, however, the majority of those who wear these do so for reasons of adornment in a pluralistic culture rather than as part of any personal belief. Similarly, in the past, when a craftsperson took a Christian motif from a textile or a pot, he or she may have done so because the design had magically protective connotations, rather than for ideological reasons. The same applies, of course, to exotic Pagan motifs.

There is much evidence of religious and artistic syncretism in the post-Roman period. For instance, at the Mark of Mote, a fortified town on the edge of Dalbeattie Forest in Kirkcudbrightshire, archaeologists have excavated cosmopolitan metalworking workshops dating from the sixth and seventh centuries. There, Celtic and Anglian craftspeople co-operated at a centre of excellence, making brooches and other small items in bronze, brass and gold. The artefacts made there incorporated contemporary elements from indigenous Celtic art, as well as Germanic motifs and interlace patterns from the eastern Mediterranean. Glass was brought in from Germanic workshops elsewhere, for use in enamel-making. Items of Mark of Mote style were exported across the sea to Ulster. Cosmopolitan centres such as this were places where differing traditions could be integrated to produce new ideas and styles. It is to them that we must look for the formative elements which went to make up the phenomenon of the Celtic Cross.

Certain cross-slabs, made in the period before free-standing stone crosses, depict the actual cross as an element of a picture, as if the cross is standing in the landscape. Often, they stand above scenes of hunting

The cross-slab from Nash Manor, South Glamorgan, Wales, depicting a standing cross. It is similar in pattern to slabs from Dunfallandy in Scotland and Maughold, Isle of Man. *(The National Museum of Wales)*

or battle, and the otherworldly 'haunted tanglewood', in which men fight serpents and dragons. Because these representations pre-date the erection of stone crosses, then the crosses they depict must have been made of some other material, either of wood, or, in the case of small ones at least, from plaitwork made of grass, straw, rushes, osiers or hazel wands. It is indisputable that interlace patterns have their origin in the plaiting of materials, such as in ropework and basketry, hurdle-making and the braiding of hair.

Until the invention of wire fencing, wattle hurdles of woven hazel were made all over the Celtic realms. Primarily known as components of fences and screens, as early as the neolithic period, trackways of hurdles were made across swampy ground, such as the Somerset Levels. The present Irish name of Dublin, Baile átha Cliath, means 'the town of the hurdle-ford'. Wattle hurdles also served as walling elements in timberframe buildings and as fish weirs. Panels of Celtic interlace work on stone carvings resemble closely the patterns employed in wattle-weaving. Ribbonwork with a central line may depict the split hazel branches from which hurdles are woven, for the actual objects have this appearance. Each region of the British Isles has its own traditional wattle-forms, expressed through the variant weaving-patterns of the 'middle binding'. The contemporary wattle-makers of Sussex and Dorset, where the craft continues, maintain their own local traditional designs to this day. In the bardic mysteries of the Celts, wattles have yet another, hidden meaning. Describing his poetic art, the Welsh bard Taliesin wrote: 'I am a reader, I love the branches and tight wattles.' In bardic language, the wattles are a metaphor for poetic knowledge. Poems written in ogham, the bardic tree alphabet, could be presented in the form of a woven wattle, containing encoded information indecipherable to the uninitiated. Perhaps some Celtic interlaces on crosses are messages in ogham.

The better-known corn dollies and other small plaited work are made throughout the Celtic lands at certain times of year, and it is unlikely that this is not the continuation of a very ancient ancestral practice. They vary in complexity, with the simplest designs being made from only two strands, but for more complicated work four, five or even six strands are needed. In Ireland, Harvest Knots are made from the straw taken at the harvest, to be worn as buttonholes for the harvest fair. Other harvest straw emblems include the stellar 'harvest stars' and the numerous forms of corn dollies. Straw-plaiting is an ancient craft, the techniques and patterns of which have been handed down through the generations. Traditional hereditary straw-plaiters, such as the late masters Fred Mizen of Essex and Arthur 'Badsey' Davis of Worcestershire, demonstrate astonishing dexterity. Davis's master-pieces, for instance, were woven simultaneously from no fewer than 49 straws. Most European corn dollies are not so complex, being made from a spiral plait that uses five strands of straw. The straws are plaited from the base in a spiral, one over the next, gradually building up a three-dimensional body of the required shape. This is the method for making the St Bridget's Cross, which, along with the simpler but re-lated Palm Sunday crosses, is an example of plaitwork which still retains its sacred connotations.

In keeping with making a holy artefact, there are a number of pre-scriptions that must be observed in making St Bridget's Crosses. They must be made on St Bridget's Eve, after sunset on the last day of January. St Bridget's Day marks the commencement of the pastoral year. Rushes must be pulled up, not cut, and the weaving must be done sunwise, from left to right. There are a number of patterns for St Bridget's Crosses, but the most common is in the form of four equal arms, set on the edge. Putting a St Bridget's Cross above the door brings holy protection from the risk of fire and other misfortunes that might befall the household. There is also a three-armed form of the cross, the triskele, which is used today only to protect cowsheds, though it is the basis of the emblem of the Isle of Man. The plaited straw charm called *Bratóg Brighde* (Bridget's Rag) is a protection against

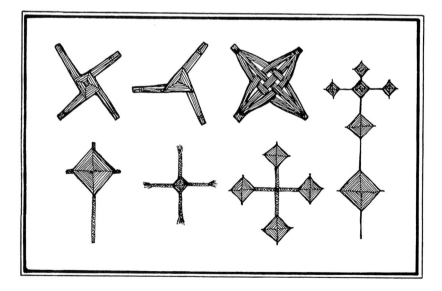

Irish St Bridget's Crosses of woven rushes (various forms).

Cross at Cardonagh, County Donegal, Ireland, where the cross has 'escaped' from the stone, but where the wheel-head is absent. The form of the interlace parallels woven crosses like those of St Bridget, though they are serpentine in form.

storms at sea, carried by the Donegal fishermen of Tory Island. Another common form that St Bridget's Cross can take is an interlace of six elements that makes a binding knot. This shows affinities with the Swabian and Tyrolean magical protector known as a *Schratterlgatterl*, which is an interweaving of a number of sticks employed as a barrier beyond which evil spirits cannot pass. Interlaces like this appear frequently in the patterns on Celtic crosses, while some Welsh and Manx crosses have designs that reproduce in stone the plaited patterns of whole crosses that are made from grass, rushes or straw, some of which are the classical Celtic Cross within the wheel. In County Galway, such 'woven crosses' are put in the rafters of the house at Hallowe'en to protect it and the family against demonic intrusion. Another form of St Bridget's Cross is in the shape of a square plaited on a cross of sticks. These straw-square patterns are made at Christmastime in Sweden and in Estonia, where they are worn on hats, and on the straw masks used in guising games.

Although they are carved from stone, many crosses have the appearance of structures made from less durable material, perhaps wickerwork or wood. Some stone crosses seem to be representations of wooden crosses upon which panels have been fixed. Therefore it is frequently suggested that many early permanent free-standing crosses were made of wood, perhaps with separate panels on the outside. Perhaps the interlace patterns on stone crosses reproduce the actual plaitwork of wickerwork that was attached both as adornment and magical protection against evil spirits. It is probable that, in Pagan days, woven sacred objects or poetic wattles resembling St Bridget's Crosses were hung on holy trees. Later, when crosses were set up, the sacred weavings were fixed to the cross instead.

In addition to panelwork made of plaited material, it is often suggested that metal panels were also used, where the patron was wealthy enough to commission them. However attractive this theory may seem, no large metal panels of this type are known, and the relative scarcity of metal in pre-industrial times makes it very unlikely that there were large wooden crosses sheathed in bronze. Attaching separate panels to larger artefacts was a common technique in Europe at that period, where craftspeople fixed cast or hammered panels bearing protective images of divine beings to helmets, armour and sacred objects. Many examples of this principle survive in the Celtic area, but they are all fairly small. They include reliquaries made to hold the possessions or holy relics of early Celtic patriarchs, such as books, bells and croziers.

Elements of woodworking technique can be seen in representations of crosses, such as the cross visible on a buttress of the church at Llangeinwen in Anglesey, or that at St Laurence's Church at Papil in Shetland. Staff-crosses ending in a spoke are depicted on slabs at Clonmacnois in County Offaly, Trowbridge in Wiltshire, and Hansted, near Aarhus in Denmark. A Celtic cross-slab re-used at a later date for part of the church fabric, the Llangeinwen cross is shown with a pointed foot, resembling a spike. It has been suggested that this shows a wooden cross, with its means of insertion in the ground, but we can never know how large this cross was meant to be. Perhaps it represents a small processional cross the size of a priest's crozier, rather than one of high-cross dimensions. There are actual contemporary illustrations of hand-held crosses for processional and ceremonial use. The north cross at Ahenny has a sculpted panel showing a funeral procession led by a priest carrying a portable wheel-headed cross. It is illustrated here. The eighth-century *Lichfield Gospels*, otherwise known as the *Gospels of St Chad*, have an illuminated page showing an evangelist holding crossed staves in the 'Osiris' position. One staff has a double-volute terminal in the manner of *Irminsul*, while the other is a Celtic Cross, with an eight-petalled pattern in the centre of the wheel. Unfortunately, the ravages of time have destroyed all of the crosses of this type, made of wood and metal, which once existed in every church.

Many of the later, larger crosses, assembled from several separate pieces of stone, were put together with mortise-and-tenon joints, which are usually associated with the craft of wood-joinery rather than that of the mainstream European tradition of stonemasonry. It can be argued, however, that because such joints in stone were used in megalithic times at Stonehenge and elsewhere, they may represent the deliberate use of an archaic technique as sacral craftsmanship. This deliberate sacred archaism appears in certain essential elements of Classical architecture. Some stone crosses, such as St Martin's Cross on Iona, also have enigmatic slots that may have accommodated wooden extensions that held ribbons, banners or woven emblems. Crosses with a circular shaft, such as the Wolverhampton Pillar and the Gosforth Cross, have patterns that resemble the tree bark left at the basal portion of some contemporary maypoles in Germany. This may recall the creation of crosses from whole trees, but equally may be derived from the patterns carved on the lower portions of Roman Jupiter Columns. Until an intact ancient wooden standing cross is found, these opposing interpretations will have equal plausibility.

OPPOSITE: Human figures depicted on Celtic Crosses. *Left: (above)* upper part of cross at Gosforth, Cumbria, England, showing an episode from the Norse prophecy of the end of this world; Ragnarök, in which Odin's son, Vidar, slays the destructive Fenris-Wolf; *(below)* Pictish cavalryman, Inchbrayock, Tayside, Scotland. *Centre:* wrestlers from the Town Cross, Kells, Meath, Ireland; mermaid from Pictish stone at Meigle, Tayside, Scotland; interlace of four men, Ahenny, Kilkenny, Ireland; monks with portable Celtic Cross, Ahenny; the Welsh warrior Briamail Flou from Llandyfaelog Fach, Powys, Wales. *Right:* quarterstaff scene, Town Cross, Kells; crucifixion scene, Gosforth, Cumbria, England.

COLOUR

Until the classical revival in the eighteenth century, it was customary in Europe to paint sculpture. In antiquity, Egyptian, Cretan and Greek sculpture was painted naturalistically, and later, in the Christian churches, images of God, Our Lady and the saints were similarly lifelike. Although in Britain we are accustomed now to seeing painted stonework only inside parish churches and cathedrals, this was not the case in former times, for all stonework was intended to be painted. The tradition continues in western Europe in the Roman Catholic church, and on the medieval gatehouses of St John's and Christ's Colleges in Cambridge. Celtic crosses were no exception. Apart from the obvious comparison with coloured manuscripts and textiles, there are traces of colour remaining on some stones, for instance the Penally Cross, and it is clear that most, if not all, crosses were originally painted in bright colours.

Forensic studies of ancient crosses have shown that, sometimes, the stone surface was prepared with an undercoat of lime whitewash or gesso, upon which the colours were painted. Like traditional fabric dyes and inks for tattooing, the colours for stone-painting were prepared from natural materials. Black and white were made from lead, red from haematite, and green from verdigris. Carved inscriptions were coloured in, as can be seen still on the Samson Cross at Llantwit Major. It is possible that the plain panels of some seemingly uninscribed stones once had painted pictures or texts. The custom of painting memorial stones with traditional materials continued in North Monmouthshire and Herefordshire until the early nineteenth century. The secret of making colours from vegetable matter and lichens was maintained in the Brute family of Llanbedr, near Crickhowell, Powys, but the recipe was lost around 1840, and the practice ceased.

Contemporary aesthetic sensibilities make it unlikely that there will be a revival of the custom of painting stones in the foreseeable future. However, in 1993, at Gosda, near Cottbus in eastern Germany, the *Runen und Bildsteinpark* was opened to the public. It is a park in which are set replicas of ancient carved and painted stones. They include Gotland memorial stones, Scandinavian ruestones and Slavonic god-stones. Currently, the *Runen und Bildsteinpark* at Gosda is the best reconstruction of how the ancient stones looked in their prime, painted in colours, and set in the landscape.

9
BRITISH CROSS STYLES

There are many examples of different styles of Celtic Cross throughout the British Isles, from Cornwall and the Isles of Scilly to Wales, the Isle of Man, northern England and Scotland. These are described in detail below.

WELSH CROSSES

There are around 450 ancient sculptured stones, crosses and allied monuments known in Wales. Stylistic analysis of surviving early stones indicates that there were individual guilds of sculptors at various important monasteries, each of which worked in their own particular recognizable styles. Thus, antiquaries have been able to identify a number of distinct schools of ancient Welsh cross sculpture. In Glamorgan, for example, there were three major workshops: at Llantwit Major, Margam and Merthyr Mawr. Their examples account for around half of the known Welsh crosses. Other recognizable sculptural workshops existed at St David's in Dyfed and at Penmon Priory on Anglesey in Gwynedd, areas that, unlike Glamorgan, were within the sphere of Irish influence. Before the ninth century, the Welsh did not use the more complex standing crosses favoured in Ireland, Scotland and the north of England. Then, under royal and ecclesiastical patronage, cross-slabs and high crosses comparable with them began to appear. Ring-headed crosses exist only in the north of Wales. Round-shafted pillar-crosses are found in north and central Wales, while wheel-crosses and allied forms are restricted to the south of the country.

The school of Glamorgan produced a characteristic form of Celtic Cross, known as the 'panelled' or 'cartwheel' slab, which were made from the late ninth century until the eleventh century. The finest example, preserved in the Margam Stones Museum, is a rectangular slab 193 cm (76 in) tall. The top half is carved with an eight-spoked

The tenth-century Conbelin Cross from Margam Abbey, south Wales. The lower part of the shaft was broken before 1690, and later the remains were re-united with the base without this portion of shaft. *(The National Museum of Wales)*

wheel, in which the spokes are arranged irregularly in pairs to make a splayed cross-pattern. There is a boss at the centre of the wheel that makes the whole composition resemble a shield. Surrounding the wheel-cross is ornamental carving containing spirals. The lower panel of the stone is inscribed with a text in Latin commemorating a certain

Ilquici. A later form of cross, which developed also on the Isle of Man, is the 'disc-headed' cross. The Margam Stones Museum keeps a fine example, though this is broken and not all of it remains. Known as the Conbelin Cross, it was found at Margam Abbey and dates from around the turn of the tenth century. Set on a rectangular stone block, which has the usual horsemen at the hunt, and just a hint of the stepped 'holy mountain' form, the shaft and disc-head were carved from a single block of Pennant Sandstone. The disc-head is sculpted with a five-square cross which overlaps the interlace-bearing ring. At the centre of the middle square is a circular boss that gives the disc the resemblance to a round shield, as with the Ilquici slab. Like some other south Welsh crosses of this period, the Conbelin cross was carved with a Latin inscription. Although damaged, it probably reads 'Conbelin set up this cross for the soul of Ric'. Inscriptions on these old Welsh crosses are often set low down, and it is possible that this is so that devotees could see them while kneeling in prayer at the foot of the crosses.

Kept in the church at Llantwit Major, under less than ideal conditions amid a jumble of chairs, tables, other carved stones and coffin lids, are no fewer than three ancestral memorials dedicated to the souls of south Welsh royalty. They are the monuments of King Samson, King Juthahel and Res, father of King Houelt. Llantwit Major, called in Welsh Llanilltyd Fawr after its founder, St Illtyd, was the sacred burial-ground of the local kings. It is a great pity that these royal memorials are not honoured properly in their own land. The Samson cross bears the words (in Latin): 'Samson set up this cross for his soul, Iltut, of Samson the King, of Samuel and Ebisar'; while the cross of King Juthahel states: 'In the name of God most high begins the Cross of the Saviour, which Abbot Samson prepared for his own soul and for the soul of King Juthahel and Artmail and Tecain.' The Houelt Cross is a cross made of local gritstone for the ruler of the local kingdom of Glywysing, Hywel ap Rhys, who was a vassal of King Alfred the Great of Wessex in the year 884. It bears the Latin inscription: 'In the name of God the Father, and of the Son, and of the Holy Spirit, this cross Houelt prepared for the soul of his father, Res.' Its supporting 'shaft' is inscribed with a tesselation of triangular key-patterns, and the wheel-head is composed of an equal-

Kept ... under less than ideal conditions amid a jumble of chairs, tables, other carved stones and coffin lids, are no fewer than three ancestral memorials dedicated to the souls of south Welsh royalty.

armed cross made from five squares, set within and overlapping a ring of single-band interlace. The four spaces between the arms of the cross are solid, and filled with three-fold interlace. Beneath a wooden awning in the churchyard at Llangan in South Glamorgan is another notable south Welsh cross-slab. Dating from around the same period as the Houelt Cross, it bears a representation of the crucifixion, of which only a few are known from this period in Wales.

Among the stones in the church at Llantwit Major is an unusual pillar, carved from sandstone. In former times, it was set in the ground outside the north wall of the church. As a pillar, it is unusual because it has a straight, vertical groove running down the back, the function of which is unknown. The zigzag and interlace patterns on the pillar are thus not continuous, but in distinct, if curved, panels. Unlike the common Celtic Cross, whose shaft is square or rectangular in cross-section, round pillars are extremely rare. There is only one other Celtic round pillar in Wales, that of Eliseg's Pillar, near Valle Crucis Abbey in north Wales. In England, the Wolverhampton Pillar is perhaps the closest parallel. These rare pillars are

Unlike the common Celtic Cross, whose shaft is square or rectangular in cross-section, round pillars are extremely rare.

the spiritual successors of the Roman columns sacred to Jupiter. Another remarkable Celtic pillar exists *in situ* in the churchyard of Llandough, near Cardiff, which is perhaps the site of the ancient monastic enclosure mentioned in 'The Life of St Cadog' (*The Lives of the British Saints*, Honourable Society of Cymmrodorion, 1908). The pillar is of a type unknown elsewhere, for it consists of four separate pieces of stone, set one upon the other. An inscription dedicates this monument to a person named Irbic. It is dated from around the millennium. The pillar's base is rather conventional. It resembles those of Irish crosses, being a rectangular pyramid with a carving of interlace, a horse and rider and a man's bust. From this rises a tapering column that has rounded pilasters carved with interlace at the four corners, with interlaced panels between them. This is topped by a small capital which supports a cushion-shaped stone whose carving makes it resemble a stack of ropes. The upper part of this cushion-stone is shaped like a cross base, and from it rises another shaft, four-sided and ornamented with interlace. The top is broken, though a similar upper portion exists nearby at Llandaff in South Glamorgan.

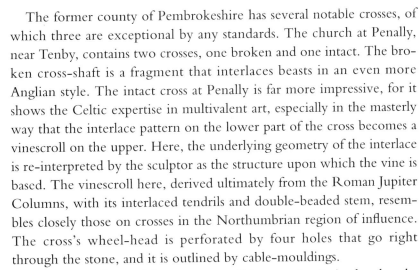

The former county of Pembrokeshire has several notable crosses, of which three are exceptional by any standards. The church at Penally, near Tenby, contains two crosses, one broken and one intact. The broken cross-shaft is a fragment that interlaces beasts in an even more Anglian style. The intact cross at Penally is far more impressive, for it shows the Celtic expertise in multivalent art, especially in the masterly way that the interlace pattern on the lower part of the cross becomes a vinescroll on the upper. Here, the underlying geometry of the interlace is re-interpreted by the sculptor as the structure upon which the vine is based. The vinescroll here, derived ultimately from the Roman Jupiter Columns, with its interlaced tendrils and double-beaded stem, resembles closely those on crosses in the Northumbrian region of influence. The cross's wheel-head is perforated by four holes that go right through the stone, and it is outlined by cable-mouldings.

The original base of the cross can still be seen *in situ* in the churchyard to the west of the church. In 1956, the Ancient Monuments Board For Wales recommended that, where possible, ancient sculptured stones and crosses should be taken indoors. Then, many stones were removed from their proper locations, marking the burial-places of the dead, to become instead indoor 'art objects'. Neither has the result of this action been a complete success. In 1995, I was told by a church warden at Penally that, since it had been removed into the church, the intact cross has deteriorated, owing possibly to the effects of heating and the smoke from candles. Although in some cases it may protect them from further erosion by polluted air, removal of crosses from their original locations not only denies the very intention of their makers, and seriously diminishes the historical reality of the place, but may also threaten the continued existence of the cross itself.

In a roadside niche in the wall surrounding the ruined Carew Castle is the 4.12-m (13½-ft) high cross dedicated, according to its inscription, to King Margiteut, son of Etguin. Known by his modern Welsh name, Meredudd ap Edwin was king of Deheubarth (this part of Wales) from 1033 to 1035. The cross is composed of two stones, the lower of which combines base and shaft. T-shaped key-patterns, diagonal knotwork, the inscription panel, irregular key-patterns and more regular looped knotwork, containing two circles. The head is made as a separate piece, like its counterpart at Nevern. Dating from around the turn of the first millennium, the Nevern churchyard cross stands 3.96 m (13 ft) high. The head of the Nevern cross, like that at Carew, was carved from a separate stone, being fixed to the shaft by means of mortise-and-tenon

The cross kept in the church at Penally, Dyfed, west Wales, in which the lower interlace patterns become the higher vinescroll, according to the same underlying geometrical scheme. The wheel-head is pierced with four holes. *(The National Museum of Wales)*

joints in the manner of Stonehenge. There are two short inscriptions, one of which reads 'DNS', being an abbreviation of the Latin word *Dominus* (Master or Lord). All four sides of the cross are illustrated here. In the church, a stained-glass window representing the founder, St Brynach, has an anachronistic representation of the Nevern Cross behind him, above which flies a dove.

Also dating from around the first millennium, and located west of Whitford in Clwyd, stands Maen Achwyfan, 'The Stone of Lamentations'. This is a monolithic cross 3.4 m (11 ft) in height. Ornamented with spirals, the X-shaped 'Pagan Cross' and irregular net-like interlace, the design of Maen Achwyfan shows affinities with Northumbrian work. The circular wheel-head is surrounded by two rings of ropelike beading, and has a cross with interlaced arms that merge with a third, inner, ring. At the very centre is a tightly interlaced central boss with a cross at the middle. One of the carvings is of an ithyphallic man.

Close to the eisteddfod town of Llangollen and the ruined Cistercian abbey of Valle Crucis (Valley of the Cross) is the Pillar of Eliseg. It has no head; only a round, treelike shaft remains. Formerly the cross had an inscription, recorded in 1696, that commemorated the erection of the cross by King Cyngen, in honour and praise of Eliseg, his great-grandfather. Cyngen, who died in the year 854, was the last king of an independent state of Powys. Today, the Pillar of Eliseg bears an inscription commemorating T. Lloyd, who, in 1779, re-erected the fallen and broken cross-shaft. On Anglesey, Penmon Priory, which may occupy the former location of the holiest shrine of the druids, contains two interesting disc-headed crosses. Dating from around the millennium, they show Norse influence, being close in their design to the crosses in the church of St John in Chester, the product of a Norse sculptural school. The motif of the temptation of St Anthony, or at least a man in combat with demons, appears on one of the crosses.

Powys has several notable cross-slabs. One of the most interesting is at Llandyfaelog Fach. Dating from the tenth century, it bears the name Briamail Flou, and has one of the few known representations of an ancient Welsh nobleman or warrior. Bearded and standing proud, Briamail holds a club across his right shoulder, while his left hand is on the hilt of a sword. Apart from being a useful weapon in the northern European martial arts, the wooden club called a *baculum* was a symbol of office. As commander-in-chief of the Norman army, William of Normandy carried one at the Battle of Hastings, as later field-marshals

ABOVE: The cross of King Meredudd ap Edwin at Carew Castle, Dyfed, Wales.

OPPOSITE: The Nevern Cross, Nevern churchyard, Dyfed, Wales. All four sides are shown. They demonstrate the inventive variations that Celtic art can take.

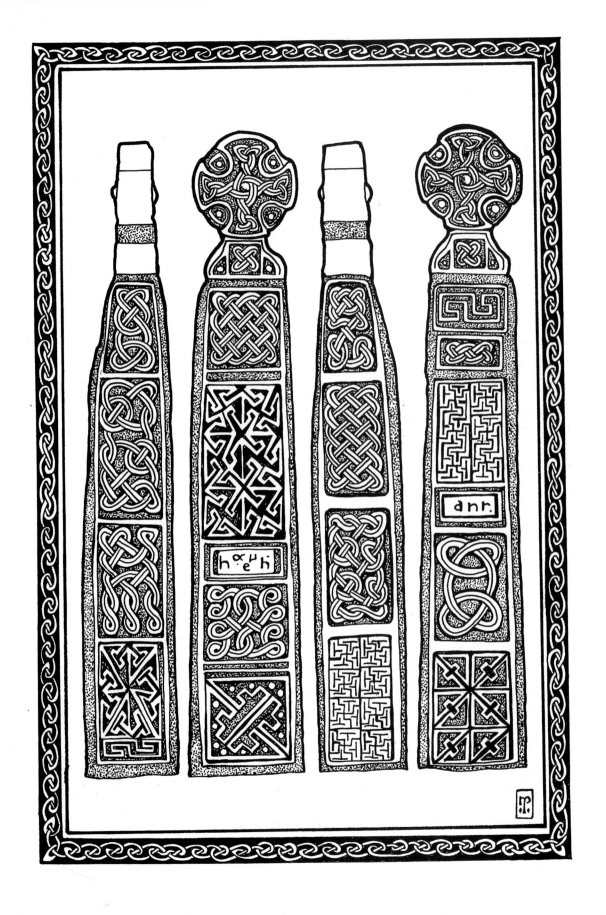

Solid-headed Celtic Cross
with angular ornament
preserved in Penmon
Priory church, Anglesey,
Wales. *(Nigel Pennick)*

carry their baton. Above Briamail is a simple cross formed of an interlaced single band. Surrounding the lord and the cross are various types
of knotwork and key-patterns, while the inscription is bordered by
ropelike banding. Another cross-slab, kept in the church at Meifod in
Powys, has a remarkable carving of a form of Christian ankh, which
resembles Coptic models. Possibly the lid of a sarcophagus, in which
case it resembles Merovingian parallels in France, it is sculpted with
two crosses. One is a conventional cross carved with interlace motifs.
At the centre of the cross is a four-fold knot with a circular middle.
Above this cross, and connected to it by a rod is a wheel-cross upon
which Christ is crucified. In the four quarters between the spokes of
the wheel are bosses. The rest of the composition is filled with knots
and beasts without any overall pattern.

The most holy Celtic Cross of Wales was the Cross Gneth, a precious reliquary that enshrined a small part of the True Cross. Formerly
in the possession of the princes of north Wales, it was taken to England
by King Edward I in 1283. When he founded the Order of the Garter

in 1348, King Edward III gave the Cross Gneth to the chapel of the Order at Windsor Castle, where it was enshrined as its most precious relic. Although the cross itself disappeared from St George's Chapel in 1548, when its gold back was sold, we know what it looked like. There is a carving of the Cross Gneth on a stone roof boss at the eastern end of the south choir aisle of the chapel. It portrays King Edward I and Bishop Beauchamp kneeling in adoration of the relic, which is a classic Celtic Cross. To all who knelt at the cross, which was taller than a man, 40 days' pardon for sins was granted.

CORNWALL AND THE ISLES OF SCILLY

It has been estimated that Cornwall has some 500 standing crosses or fragments, dating from between the ninth and the fifteenth centuries. This is a very high number for a relatively small area. More crosses seem to have survived in this county than elsewhere in England, perhaps because of its Celtic traditions where sacred places belonged to families rather than the church. In parts of England and Wales where the Celtic tradition had been weakened or extirpated, crosses belonged to the church, and when Roman Catholicism was suppressed at the Reformation they were destroyed. In predominantly Celtic areas like Cornwall, however, individual crosses actually belonged to individual families, and could not so easily be pulled down.

Cornish crosses tend to be rather simpler than those in other parts of the British Isles, owing perhaps to the hardness of the local stone – granite – that was used to make them. They have three distinct types. Some are round-headed pillar-stones; others are Latin crosses carved from a single stone; others are wheel-headed crosses, often drilled through with four holes between the arms. Of the round-headed variety, there are ten main types of carved cross – six use crosses within circles, and the others have various unencircled kinds of cross carved onto them. Some round-headed cross-pillars are carved with the crucified Christ, but without a cross.

Because Cornwall was not conquered by the Anglo-Saxons until the year 925, it retained the older Romanized Celtic culture, maintaining links by sea with Wales to the north, the Isles of Scilly to the west and Brittany to the south.

The positions of the body vary greatly, and comparable figures exist on wheel-headed crosses. Many of the later crosses have Celtic interlace patterns comparable with known examples in other parts of the British

Isles, as well as geometric ornament that resembles Anglo-Norman grave-slab work in England and Wales. The variety of Cornish crosses is a remarkable tribute to the inventiveness of their artists.

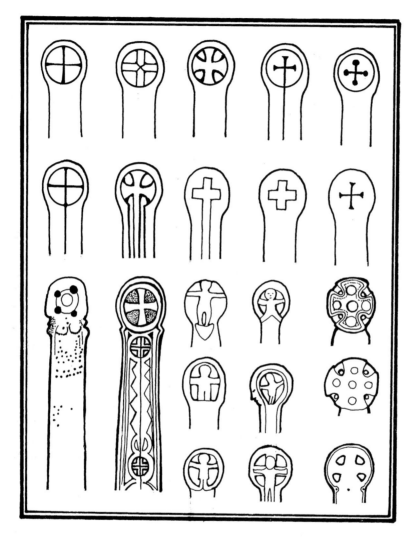

Variant forms of Cornish crosses.
Top row, left to right: Camborne; Crowan; Helston; Tintagel; Budock.
Second row: Pradannack; St Buryan; St Wendron; St Dennis; Michaelstow.
Third row: Merthyr Uny; Scorrier, St Day; Trevolis, Stythians; Pendarves, Camborne; St Paul.
Fourth row: Clowance; Trevean, St Erth; St Erth.
Fifth row: St Erth; St Just; Penlee, Penzance.

Most surviving Cornish crosses date from between the eleventh and thirteenth centuries. In the thirteenth century, there was a resurgence of crossmaking in the older style, such as the cross at Quethioc, where medieval 'gothic' influence is modified by simplified vinescroll patterns. Because Cornwall was not conquered by the Anglo-Saxons until the year 925, it retained the older Romanized Celtic culture, maintaining links by sea with Wales to the north, the Isles of Scilly to the west and Brittany to the south. Cornwall thus has a number of wheel-head crosses the designs of which are related to those in south Wales, which may even have been made by sculptors trained there. In some cases, individual patterns may occur in both places. For example, the pattern of a Cornish interlace cross at Cardinham, composed of four triquetra knots, is identical to those at Coychurch in South Glamorgan and Nevern in Dyfed. Also, the monasteries of St Buryan near Land's End and St Petroc at Bodmin appear to have had schools of sculptors like those identified in south Wales. In the Bodmin area, a series of crosses was set up around the monastery of St Petroc, which was flourishing in the tenth century. In the most notable of these, which stands at Cardinham, the sculptor used a variety of motifs, running spirals, ring-loop interlace and a ring-chain that fades into a rectilinear meander pattern. The ring-chain is a motif the oldest known example of which is the cross at Michael, Isle of Man, which was carved by the tenth-century runemaster-sculptor Gaut Bjornsson.

As in other Celtic countries, stopping-places along paths, pilgrimage roads and trackways in Cornwall were marked by wayside crosses. The custom was maintained for many centuries, and as late as 1447 the Rector of the parish of Creed left money in his will to pay for the erection of new stone crosses in the county at stopping-places 'where dead bodies are rested on their way to burial, that prayers be made, and the bearers take some rest.' Churchyard crosses dating from the ninth and tenth centuries were often located to the right of the church entrance, and, as in the rest of northern Europe, there was a tradition of erecting crosses in market-places. Two tenth-century wheel-head crosses stand in Sancreed churchyard, both with representations of the crucifixion at the centre of the wheel-head. One bears the name Runhol, whose name is also discernible on a cross that stands near the door of Lanherne Convent. Formerly, this cross was in the parish of Gwinear, but, as is the case with so many crosses, it was moved.

The remains of a royal cross stand near the road to Liskeard about 1.6 km (1 mile) northwest of St Cleer. Reduced by breakage to part of a cross-shaft, the remains bear an inscription commemorating Doniert, who was King of Cornwall around the year 875. Close to the celebrated 'lost church' of St Piran at Perranporth stands a cross that is mentioned in a charter dating from the year 960. Unlike the majority of Celtic Crosses, it has pecked ornament rather than interlace or key-patterns. Its most notable feature, however, shows it to be a direct continuation of the older Pagan wheel-headed stones of the Celts, for its wheel-head is not a vertical Christian cross but an X-shape, with the four holes cut on the vertical and horizontal axes. Thus, it can be said that, technically, this ancient stone is not a cross at all but an instance of the older, Pagan, tradition of the continental Celts.

The crosses of the Isles of Scilly closely resemble those in Cornwall. Three ancient shaped granite crosses exist within the oval churchyard at St Buryan, originally an Irish settlement, while at St Mary's an old high cross serves as a gable cross on the church at Old Town. Two crosses once stood as boundary-markers on the site of the present St Mary's airport, and one of them, from High Cross Lane, Salakee, was removed in 1887 to St Mary's Church. During the nineteenth century, many of the crosses of the Isles of Scilly were taken away from their original positions by collectors. For example, in the nineteenth century, Mr E. N. V. Moyle, the Clerk to the Council of the Isles of Scilly, used his position of influence to assemble a notable collection of stones, including crosses, in his garden at Rocky Hill, St Mary's. It is arguable that the crosses were saved from destruction by their removal, but equally the disrespect for the sacred that allowed holy stones to be taken away for personal pleasure is a sign that a spiritual understanding of the landscape was already in decline.

THE ANGLO-SAXON TRADITION

Around 2,500 pieces of Anglo-Saxon sculpture are known from England and southern Scotland. When they immigrated into Britain, the Angles and Saxons were Pagan, but they came under the influence of Celtic Christianity when Irish missionaries arrived to found monasteries in Wessex and Northumbria. Later, Roman Catholic missions came from the continent, and it was this influence which proved more lasting. In Northumbria, Benedict Biscop and Wilfrid brought in stonemasons and glaziers from Gaul and Rome to build churches and make artefacts, including, most probably, stone crosses. The designs on the earliest Northumbrian crosses have affinities with Egyptian and Syrian sources, and it is likely that their sculptors were trained outside the British Isles. The earliest of these Anglo-Saxon high crosses are at Bewcastle, Easby, Hexham, Otley and Ruthwell. They are all in the form of tapered cross-shafts sculpted with panels containing religious figures and ornament. The Bewcastle cross has a runic inscription that has been interpreted as being either a memorial to King Alcfrith or commemorating the Christianization of Cumbria by force of arms, around the year 670.

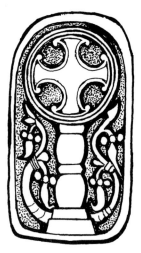

Anglo-Saxon cross-slab from Hanley Castle, Hereford and Worcester, England.

The fragments of a Northumbrian cross that commemorates Wilfrid's successor, Acca, can be seen at Hexham in Northumberland. According to the *Historia Regum* of the twelfth-century chronicler Symeon of Durham, Bishop Acca, who died in 740, was buried outside the east wall of Hexham Church. His grave was marked by two wonderfully carved crosses, one set up at the head and the other at the foot.

The designs on the earliest Northumbrian crosses have affinities with Egyptian and Syrian sources, and it is likely that their sculptors were trained outside the British Isles.

They bore the inscription that Acca was buried there. The crosses were smashed at a later date, and only fragments were recovered. At the Reformation and in Cromwell's wars, most of the surviving Anglo-Saxon crosses suffered attacks from Protestant extremists, who, considering them to be symbols of 'Popery and superstition', smashed them with religious zeal. Even the best crosses did not escape. In the seventeenth century, one of the finest, at Ruthwell, was pulled down and broken up by activists following a Church of Scotland edict concerning 'idolatrous monuments in the kirk of Ruthwell'. Those we see today have been either re-erected or re-assembled from broken pieces.

The only Anglo-Saxon cross still retaining its original head is at Irton in Lancashire. It is similar in form to the Irish high crosses, but, in common with its Anglian counterparts, does not have a wheel-head. A fine full-sized replica of it can be seen in the Victoria and Albert Museum in London. In addition to the Northumbrian school, there were separate schools of crossmaking in the other Anglian and Saxon kingdoms. The finest examples of Mercian crosses can be seen at Sandbach in Cheshire and at Bakewell and its environs. A school of cross-sculptors has been identified in Derbyshire at Bakewell, from which 65 examples, in various states of preservation, are known. Later Mercian crosses were refined into a form close to the classical Celtic wheel-head, by the addition of a ring.

Following Pagan practice, the Celtic church used mark-stones to sanctify crossing-places, such as fords and bridges and the entrances to holy enclosures. This practice was transmitted by Irish priests to the Anglo-Saxon church, through which it became part of the sacred landscape of England. Perhaps the most powerful instance of the cross as boundary-marker was at Beverley in Humberside (formerly Yorkshire), which in former times was one of the most holy places of England.

The minster was given its rights in the year 937 by King Athelstan after he had borrowed the standard of St John of Beverley to use as his holy war-banner at the Battle of Brunanburgh where his greatly outnumbered English army defeated the combined forces of the Celto-Danish confederation. In the Beverley charter, Athelstan stated: 'In your church shall be a college of canons, endowed with ample possessions. It shall be a sanctuary, with a Frithstool before the altar, as a place of refuge and safety for debtors and criminals. Four stones, each a mile distant from this place, shall mark the bounds of the privileged ground. Your monastery shall be extended, and revenues increased, and the shrine of the Blessed John be amongst the most magnificent in the land.' King Athelstan was a promoter of the craft of masonry, which, as the masonic *Regius Poem* (c. 1400), tells us: 'came into England ... in the time of good King Athelstan's day.' Clearly, it was these masons who sculpted and erected Athelstan's stone crosses.

Standing stone crosses were the significant markers in Athelstan's geomantic layout of the Beverley sanctuary. Originally, the holy ground extended 2.5 km (1½ miles) in every direction from the Minster. The area within this was divided into a number of concentric enclosures of increasing sanctity, of which there were two main areas, one inside the other. The entry-points into the Outer and the Second at the north, east, south and west were marked by stone crosses, three of which still exist. The churchyard wall was the third boundary, inside which the western church door was the fourth. The next boundary-

LEFT: A fragment of cross from Gosforth in Cumbria, England, with a scene depicting the giant Hymir and the god Thor fishing in the Atlantic for the world serpent Jörmungand, using an ox-head as bait. This story is from the Pagan scriptures known as *The Edda*.

OPPOSITE: The binding of Loki in the underworld, a carving from an Anglo-Scandinavian cross-fragment at Kirkby Stephen, Cumbria, England.

line came at the choir screen inside the church, and the sixth was the frithstool itself. This was a stone throne in which the fugitive from justice had to sit in order to claim sanctuary. Violators of the sanctuary were punished with an increasing scale of fines, beginning with the outer boundary with a fine of one Hundredth (£8), being doubled at the next cross and so on as far as the frithstool in the inner sanctum. Violators of the frithstool itself, however, were declared outlaws and punished with death. Similar enclosures, marked by crosses at the four quarters, existed around holy places in Ireland, Scotland and Wales.

THE ISLE OF MAN

Situated between Britain and Ireland, and with a history of being first an independent Celtic island, then a Norse kingdom, the Isle of Man has its own unique crosses. As other Celtic countries, the earliest Manx crosses are inscribed standing stones, some of which bear inscriptions in ogham or Roman script. Some of these memorial stones are bilingual. One, at Knoc-y-doonee, Andreas, which dates from the sixth century, had on one face the Latin *Ammecat filius Rocat hic jacet* (Ambecatos son of Rocatos lies here), and on the left side the fragmental ogham Celtic inscription *(Am)b(e)catos maqi Rocatos*. A standing stone from Maughold is interesting in being a transitional form from the standing memorial stone to the classical Celtic Cross. Inside a circle surrounded by an inscription in the manner of a seal is a hexafoli pattern that was the sigil of the goddess Juno in Roman religion. Beneath the Pagan goddess sigil are two *chi-rho* crosses with accompanying inscriptions.

The crosses of the Isle of Man developed in the same broad way as in other Celtic and Celtic-influenced areas. From the simple cross-inscribed standing stone developed the cross-slab with complex carvings, representing a standing cross amid ornament or mythic scenes. One of the most evocative Celtic crucifixion scenes is on a Manx stone of this type. Although it is a broken fragment, the remains of a late eighth-century slab from the Calf of Man depicts Christ on the cross, with Longinus about to spear him. Christ is richly dressed, with a roundel of interlace over his heart. Remarkable though this is, it is outside the mainstream of designs of Manx crosses. Another of the crosses at Maughold resembles Pictish examples, having a carving of a

ABOVE: A representation of the crucifixion on a slab from the Calf of Man. (*Manx National Heritage*)

OPPOSITE: Reconstructions from fragments of crosses from Kirk Conchan, Isle of Man, showing 'wicker-work' interlace and guardian dogs of Conchem/St Christopher.

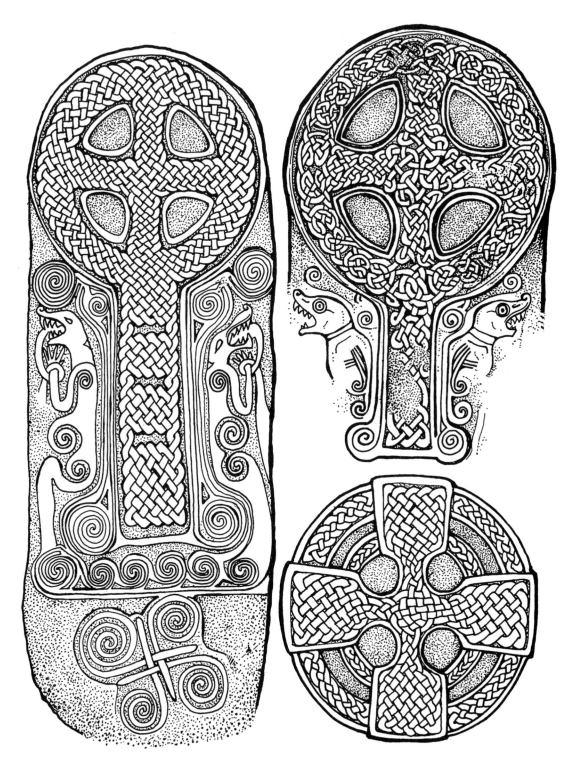

wheel-head cross, on either side of which is a seated monkish figure, representing Paul and Anthony, a popular theme in the Celtic church.

The 'boss' or 'serpent stone' style of the Pictish stones and the western Scottish and Irish crosses also appeared in the Isle of Man. At Maughold, Crux Guriat is a flat slab which has five bosses in a cross-pattern, carved just inside the ring of a wheel-head. The bosses, however, are in a much lower relief than those elsewhere and are not carved with the 'serpent's egg' interlace patterns. Furthermore, there is no actual cross within the circle. Unlike Crux Guriat, the Conchan crosses (see page 113) known by their prosaic catalogue numbers 92 and 93, are the forerunners of the free-standing stone crosses. Although they are slabs carved with crosses and beasts, it is likely that the tops of the stones were rounded to conform with the outline of the wheel-cross. In these two crosses, the wheel-head, cross and shaft are all composed of continuous interlace patterns, resembling nothing less than crosses composed entirely of wickerwork. Like others of this kind in Scotland, they give us the impression that the whole cross-slab is a picture of a free-standing cross in the land. Perhaps they represent wooden or wickerwork crosses that have not survived. The other Conchan cross illustrated (No. 74) is closer to the Irish tradition, where the cross-part and wheel-part are separated, as though the wheel is behind the cross as its support rather than integral with it. The form of cross where the stone has been shaped into a rounded form outlining the wheel, supported on a wide base like those at Llantwit Major and Margam, is also known in the Isle of Man, for example in a cross from Kirk Braddan and another at Lonan, which has the close, wickerlike interlace of the Conchan crosses. The next step in this development came when the cross 'escaped' entirely from the slab, and the free-standing stone Celtic Cross was born.

Under Norse rulership, which initially was Pagan, syncretic religious practices evolved, in which Christian and Pagan elements which had the same symbolic meaning co-existed alongisde one another. Thus, Odin, Thor, Heimdall and other gods of the northern pantheon were carved by the Northmen. Also, the spirits of the land, rarely present in other Celtic crosses, the dwarfs, gnomes, trolls, giants and dragons, made their appearance on the Northmen's crosses in Man. These Manx crosses are important mythologically, for they depict several significant episodes from Norse sacred stories, including elements recognizable from the Pagan scriptures known as *The Edda*. Episodes from the life of the hero Sigurd Fafnirsbane are depicted on a number of Manx crosses,

OPPOSITE: Manx cross-fragments with episodes from Norse religion.
Top row, left to right: Thor Cross, Kirk Bride, with beasts and shield-knot; Kirk Maughold, with beasts trampling corpse; Malew, fragment with episode from the legend of Sigurd Fafnirsbane the dragon-slayer.
Lower row: cross-slab from Jurby, with carving of Heimdall/Gabriel with his horn of summoning; wheel-head with Odin and the wolves (Daniel in the lions' den).

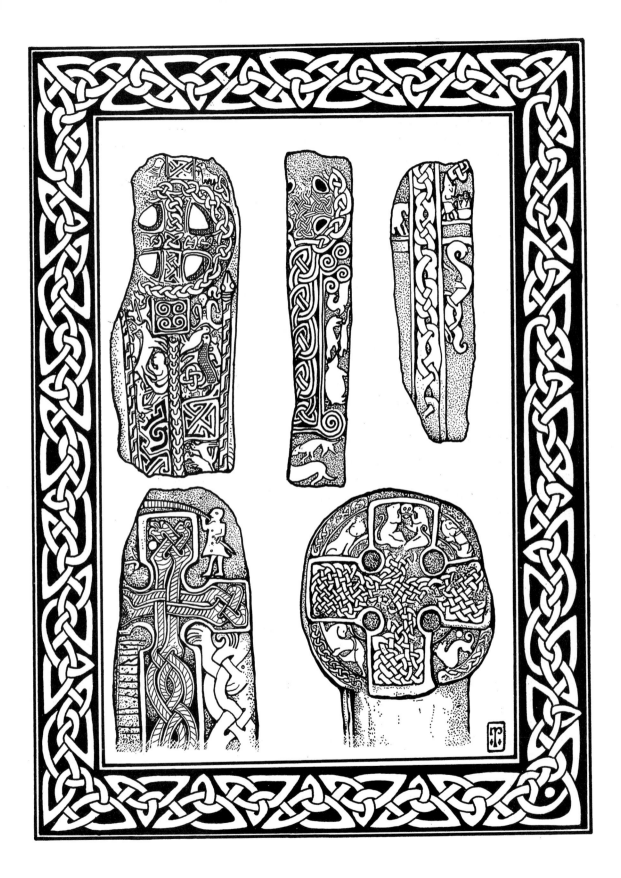

most notably those from Jurby, Malew and Maughold. The broken cross from Jurby shows the hero Sigurd, Wagner's Siegfried, killing the dragon Fafnir. Another cross from Jurby shows the Rainbow Bridge, Bifröst, with Heimdall the warder of Asgard sounding the Gjallarhorn to summon all the gods to battle against the forces of destruction. On a cross thought to be the memorial of King Olaf the Red, who was killed at Ramsey in 1153, are depictions of the story of the trickster-god Loki. The Kirk Bride cross depicts the four dwarfs that hold up the sky in Norse cosmology, Nordri, Ostri, Sudri and Vestri;

Under Norse rulership … syncretic religious practices evolved, in which Christian and Pagan elements which had the same symbolic meaning co-existed alongside one another.

a figure with a staff, perhaps Odin; Thor, fighting the World Serpent; and the giant Rungnir. On a slab from Andreas, we can see Odin in combat with the Fenris-Wolf. Like the Cumbrian Gosforth Cross, the Manx crosses of the Norse period are wonderful examples of 'dual faith' religious syncretism, where archetypal myths of different systems coexist in perfect harmony.

Eighth-century Anglian runes have been found on the remains of crosses at Maughold, spelling out the names Blagc-Mon and ---gmon. Both crosses have an early form of the cross pattee inscribed inside a circle, with remains of the Greek letters *alpha* and *omega*. Other runic inscriptions on Manx crosses are in the later Scandinavian runes of the tenth to thirteenth centuries. A stone found at Kirk Maughold bears an invocation in thirteenth-century runes: 'Krist: Malaki and Patrick: Adamnan: But of all the sheep Iuan is the priest in Kurna valley.' Although this runic inscription appears to be in honour of a Christian priest, when we encounter runic invocations to the saints it was not necessarily Christians who carved them. The process of making saints in the church is identical to the apotheosis of Pagan heroes who enter the pantheon to become divine, in the manner of Hercules or Alexander the Great. It is only according to the theological doctrine of the Christian religion that they do not become gods. Yet, like their Pagan counterparts, they also enter the otherworldly realms, from which they may be invoked to grant aid to human beings. Recognizing this, the Pagan Danes in Ireland invoked St Patrick as the god of the land in their struggles against the Norwegians there. As recorded in the Irish *Annals* of Mac Firbis: 'This St Patrick, against whom these enemies of ours have committed many evils, is archbishop and head of the saints of Erin. Let us pray to him fervently and let us give alms to him honourably for gaining victory and triumph over our enemies.'

OUTSIDE THE BRITISH ISLES

The Celtic Cross form is not unknown outside the British Isles, though its connection with the Celts may be tenuous or fortuitous, for occurrences are few and far between. In the late medieval period, small wayside crosses with wheel-heads about a metre (3 ft) in diameter were erected in parts of Germany. The example illustrated here is from Calden, near Kassel. Also, in southwestern France and northern Spain, the traditional Basque tombstones, known as *estela discoidea*, include wheel-crosses as well as eight-fold wheels and hexagrams. Perhaps more closely related to the authentic Celtic tradition was an intriguing cross illustrated by the Danish antiquary Ole Worm in 1651 in Book Six of his *Danicorum Monumentorum*. This stone cross stood at Julskovkorset on the island of Fünen. It was in the form of a wheel-headed high cross that bore the inscription: 'In the year 1445 Wolfgang and his son Oluf had these letters chiselled.' A labyrinth was carved on the cross-shaft. Unfortunately, this remarkable high cross no longer exists. During the nineteenth century, the influence of the Celtic revival saw the erection of Celtic Crosses wherever there was British influence. In Brittany, a small British-style Celtic Cross was set up as a finial on the holy well at St Cado.

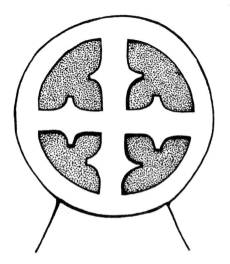

A medieval stone cross from Calden, near Kassel, Germany. The whole cross is sculptural; the cross-pattern is carved in relief without piercing the stone.

10
IRISH HIGH CROSSES

The symbolic structure of the fully developed wheel-head Celtic Cross can be seen as representative of the *axis mundi* or cosmic axis. According to Welsh bardic traditions recorded in the middle ages, and taught by contemporary druidism, the cosmos is conceived as having several 'circles' or levels, which can be visualized as if they were stacked one on top of the other along an axis. Like *Irminsul*, this axis is the subtle link between the underworld below, through the middle earth on which we live, to the heavenly upperworld above. At birth, death and under some other special conditions during life, spirits migrate between these worlds. The Celtic Cross is conceived in terms of the bardic cosmic axis, which in contemporary psychological terms sees the base of the cross symbolizing the unconscious, the shaft the ascending consciousness, and the top transcendence.

THE COSMIC DIMENSION

According to the Welsh spiritual tradition, the underworld is called Annwn, the middle world Abred, and the upper world Gwynvyd. A Welsh bardic text called *Y Tri Chyflwr* (The Three States) tells us: 'According to the three principal qualities of man shall be his migration in Abred; from laziness and mental blindness he shall fall to Annwn; from dissolute wantonness he shall traverse the circle of Abred, according to his necessity; and from his love for goodness he will ascend to the circle of Gwynvyd.' This idea is broadly in accord with the three Christian worlds of Hell, Earth and Heaven, though bardic tradition infers many journeys within the system through re-incarnation. These three worlds represent spiritual progress: 'The three states of living beings: Annwn, from which comes the beginning; Abred, in which knowledge increases, and hence goodness; and Gwynvyd, in which is the plenitude of goodness, knowledge, truth and endless life.'

OPPOSITE: The cosmic axis, according to Welsh bardic tradition. At the lowest level is Annwn. Above this is middle earth, Abred, with the eight directions and the central *omphalos* stone or cross. Overlying Abred is Gwynvyd, the heavenly 'White Land'. Finally, above that is Ceugant, the ineffable realm of deity. Behind are the underlying patterns of *manred*.

Although the underworld is conceived as a place of the dead, it is not so much the infernal burning place of devilish torture of the Judaeo-Christian scriptures. Rather it resembles the Greek Hades as the gloomy abode of insubstantial shadows. Thus, itis called variously *affan*, the land invisible, *affwys*, the abyss, and *annwyn* or *annwfn*, the not-world. According to a bardic question-and-answer fragment, recorded in *Barddas*: '*Question*. In what place is Annwyn? *Answer*. Where there is the least possible of animation and life, and the greatest of death, without other condition.' Thus, the soil of the graveyard, in which the cross stands, is truly Annwn. Many high crosses are set on steps or a four-square pyramidal base, both of which are representations of the archetypal world mountain, inside which is the realm of the dead. The stepped bases or *perrons* recall the much more ancient step-pyramids and ziggurats of Egypt and Babylon whose terraces led upwards to a summit platform upon which the image of divinity was set. Powerful examples of stepped cross-bases exist at Llantwit Major and St David's in Wales, at Kildalton on Islay and Clackmannan in Scotland. Pagan forerunners of these cross-bases exist in Ireland at Mullaghmast in County Kildare and at Killycluggan in County Cavan. Classic examples of the four-square pyramidal cross-base exist in Ireland at Ahenny, Castledermot and Monasterboice, while an intermediate form of stepped base supports St Martin's Cross on Iona. Their raised bases recall the earlier grave-mounds which were literally the abodes of the dead from which rose the axial memorial stone that pointed towards the heavens. According to Celtic folk-lore, these mounds are places where sensitive people can commune with the spirits of the departed. In his 1703 book *Gweledigaetheu y Bardd Cwsc*, Ellis Wynne describes three visions of this world, death and Hell, where the sleeping bard sees a vision of the dead, the Children of Annwn, dancing upon the churchyard mound. Celtic lore such as these reminds us that such mounds are not only places of burial but also places of vision, where one may glimpse the spirits of the otherworld.

The stepped bases or 'perrons' recall the much more ancient step-pyramids and ziggurats of Egypt and Babylon whose terraces led upwards to a summit platform upon which the image of divinity was set.

Above the basal 'mound', the cosmic axis of the cross rises from the underworld into this world of living mortals, Abred. The axis leads ever upwards from middle earth to the heavenly upperworld, called in the bardic tradition The Circle of Gwynvyd, the 'White Land'. This is the bright realm represented as the wheel-cross, emblem of the sun above the earth as the symbol of the sky god, upon which the Christ is manifest. According to Breton beliefs, the cross of Christ is envisaged as a ladder from earth to heaven, down which God came to earth. By means of this divine ladder to heaven, human souls are enabled to climb to paradise. From the sixteenth century, when Breton priests began to re-consecrate prehistoric megaliths, it was customary to carve them with the symbols of the passion of Christ, which include a ladder.

Although crosses often end with the upper arm of the wheel-head, the most highly developed among them are topped by a little house which in bardic cosmology represents the heavenly throne or mansion of God, Ceugant. The most striking example is on top of Muiredach's Cross at Monasterboice. The capstone of the cross from Tihilly in County Offaly, preserved at University College in Dublin, is also house-shaped, as were probably the missing capstones of the crosses at Cloonfad and Duleek. The existing cross-top houses closely resemble known portable reliquaries, the small, highly decorated boxes in which holy relics, whether the bones of a saint, his book or some other sacred item, were kept. The *Annals of Ulster* tell of how the relics of Conlaed were placed in a shrine made of gold and silver, which coincides with the dating of Irish house-shrines from the eighth or ninth century. The *Annals of Clonmacnois* record that in 1129 among the relics stolen from the monastic altar was a reliquary in the form of a model of Solomon's Temple in Jerusalem, which in Judaeo-Christian tradition was the reflection of the heavenly mansion of God on Earth. The *Book of Kells* shows us the Irish idea of what the Jerusalem Temple looked like. It is depicted in a representation of the Temptation of Christ by the Devil. Christ is on the ridge of a steeply gabled roof which is covered with tiles or shingles and adorned with serpents'-head finials. The temple walls are similarly adorned with scales or ornamented panels.

A number of these jewelled miniature houses have come down to us through the centuries because of the excellent Celtic custom that relics are preserved by hereditary keepers. Among the finest are the Monymusk Reliquary in the National Museum of Scotland in Edinburgh, and the Emly Shrine. Dating from the year 800, the latter is kept in the Museum of Fine Arts in Boston, Massachusetts. Others, taken as booty by Viking raiders, and later buried with their new owners, re-emerged from archaeological excavations in recent times. The museums at Copenhagen and Trondheim house notable examples.

They are all eloquent testimony to the exquisite artistry and craftsmanship of their makers.

Irish holy objects show a repetition of house shapes ranging from those large enough for a human being to enter to those small enough to hold in one hand. This repeating hierarchy is a classic instance of the Celtic concept of self-similarity. According to this hierarchical system, the unseen universal Mansion of God is the largest, within that the church, then the reliquary-tomb and finally, within it, the metal reliquary itself.

Several surviving ancient Irish churches show the prototype for the house-shrines. The pilgrimage church on St MacDara's Island in County Galway is one of the best examples, having been restored recently with its original roof-ornament of Y-shaped gable finials. The church at Killinaboy in County Clare bears a cross on its west end that recalls the reliquary of the True Cross once kept inside. Inside some churches were reliquary-tombs whose form reflected the churches in which they stood. Extant examples are the reliquary-tombs at Banagher in County Londonderry, Saul in County Down, Clones in County Monaghan and the Skull House at Cooley in County Donegal. They are all in the form of houses of the dead, the so-called 'mortuary houses'. The Clones mortuary house, which probably contained relics of St Tighernach, has gable finials, once stood inside a church, now destroyed. Inside such stone shrines, smaller wooden or metal ones may have been deposited. The small metal Lough Erne Shrine, actually demonstrates the principle of self-similarity by containing a small shrine within a larger one of the same form. The practice of carving a representation of the crucifixion upon a cross, where Christ is shown on another cross, is yet another instance of Celtic self-similarity.

Because, according to Christian cosmology, the souls of those who die blameless go to live in the heavenly house at the apex of the cosmos, the houses on top of Celtic crosses are an expression of this belief. It is not just a Christian concept, however, for it exists also in Nordic cosmology, where the house of the dead symbolizes the great hall of Odin, Valhalla. The flowering of the Irish high cross came after contact with the Pagan cosmology of the Northmen, for the house of the dead was an important element in Germanic and Norse belief. The Anglo-Saxon chronicler, Bede, recounts that the memorial of St Chad, who died in the year 670, was made of wood in the shape of a gabled house. Also, the two known wooden coffins of seventh-century Archbishops of Canterbury were also both in the form of the house of the dead: one had a hipped roof with a convex section, and the other had a high-pitched gabled roof.

The Anglo-Saxon Hedda Stone in Peterborough Cathedral is a more durable example of the Canterbury wooden coffins, being in the form of a carved stone house-tomb 1.5 m (5 ft) in length. It has a roof sculpted with birds, beasts and interlace, while the walls below are arcaded with figures standing in each niche or doorway. These doors with guardian figures recall the Norse accounts of the many doorways of Valhalla. According to *The Edda*, from the 540 doors of the Allfather's hall come the dead, in the shape of the Einherjar, Odin's heroes, to fight against the powers of evil and destruction. Unfortunately, a few years ago, during building works in the cathedral, the Hedda stone was handled carelessly and damaged by having parts broken off it. The cast in the Victoria and Albert Museum shows the condition of the stone before this incident. Another important surviving house-shrine tomb is the Kentish Fordwich stone, which is believed to have originated in Canterbury. About the same length as the Hedda Stone, it is in the form of a building with a slightly curving pitched roof, carved with 'beaver-tail' tiles, and with walls sculpted as an arcade in the Romanesque manner.

In parts of England and southern Scotland are a number of recumbent stone grave-markers known by the generic term of 'hogsback tombstones'. Associated mainly with areas of Norse settlement, they are made in the form of a Scandinavian house of the time, generally boat-shaped with flattened ends like a Cambridge punt. Although it is possible that they recall ship-burials, their form is primarily the 'house of the dead'. The form of these houses of the dead is taken from the Nordic timber-framed houses whose frame structure was based upon the cruck principle rather than the box-frame. Hogsbacks are a direct development of the pagan *omphalos*-shaped bauta-stones that were erected on grave-mounds. These houses are depicted as having a tiled roof, whose ridge is sometimes the spine of a dragon or a serpent, resembling the coffins of the Alamanni, which were carved from tree-trunks. Beneath the roof are the walls, which in some cases bear interlace patterns, and in others, warriors. There is a Nordic folk tradition that the walls of the house of the dead were woven from snakes, and its form also resembles the wickerwork coffins used in former times in some areas. A hogsback, formerly at the old Anglian royal place of Repton in Derbyshire, had spiralling serpents carved on its walls. Unfortunately, it was broken up early in the nineteenth century.

A hogsback in Durham Cathedral Library has its ends protected by bears with bands around their muzzles, grasping and supporting the roof-ridge of the house. Almost identical houses of the dead are kept in the church at Brompton in North Yorkshire, where there were once ten such examples. Similar bear-stones are known from Lowther in Cumbria and Heysham in Lancashire. A fragment of hogsback from the Hospitium at York shows that its sides were composed of carved interlace and scrollwork, over which was a representation of a shingled roof. The churchyard at Penrith in Cumbria contains four such tiled-roof stones, and there are similar ones at Deerness in Orkney and St Boniface's churchyard on Papa Westray. A stone of this type from Falstone in Northumberland has a double inscription in Anglo-Saxon and runic letters on the walls, which are scribed into parallel lines like wooden boards. Other fine examples exist at Sockburn in County Durham and Govan in Glasgow. One of the Govan stones is in the form of a beast, where the roof-tiles are interpreted as scales, while another has a serpent as the roof-ridge, with the tile-pattern appearing as many small doors, recalling those of Valhalla. It is clear from all of these British instances that both the Celtic reliquaries and the Nordic houses of the dead are part of the same tradition as the houses carved on top of the Irish high crosses.

A 'house of the dead' memorial stone with inscriptions from Falstone, Northumberland, England.

THE HIGH CROSSES OF IRELAND

The Celtic Cross attained its most refined form in Ireland in the shape of the high cross, and we are fortunate that the ravages of Puritan zealots were less thorough there than in Great Britain. Many excellent ancient crosses survive, some even in their original locations. Only their colour is lost, and, with the effects of time and weather, some of them are eroded. Nevertheless, they provide wonderful examples of the high level of skill and artistry of their makers. However, we should not lose sight of the fact that many ancient crosses have been destroyed, and those that remain are only part of the story of the Celtic Cross.

Stylistically, seven classes have been identified by commentators, but, surprisingly, there are no high crosses in the south and west of Ireland. The first class of high cross is the Ahenny group. The two fine crosses at Ahenny in Tipperary are considered to be the earliest existing examples of Irish free-standing wheel-head crosses. Dating from some time soon after the year 700, they have relatively little figurative sculpture. At Ahenny, the South Cross is carved with spirals and interlace. There are also five bosses, one for each of the arms of the cross, and one marking the centre. On top of both of the Ahenny crosses are tapering cylindrical caps that resemble the tops of some Slavonic Pagan pillar-stones. Another notable cross of the Ahenny kind is at Kiltieran.

The second class is the Bealin Group. Named after the cross-fragment at Bealin in Westmeath, which has a round, shieldlike centre, this group includes the North Cross at Clonmacnois. Dating from the late eighth or early ninth centuries, these crosses have interlace and spiral ornament, and some images of horsemen. The third group includes the crosses at Castledermot, Moone and Old Kilcullen, all in County Kildare. Like those of the Bealin Group, they date from the late eighth or the early ninth centuries. They are good examples of the playful way that the crossmakers used mixed motifs with classical Celtic inventiveness. The eastern sides of the two crosses at Castledermot have crucifixion scenes at the centre of the wheel-head, for it is customary for the crucifixions depicted on Celtic Crosses to face towards the east. The South Cross at Castledermot mixes panels depicting human scenes with interlace and spirals. The east face has human panels, while the west is interlace. There is a notable depiction of the patron of monks, St Anthony of Egypt, in combat with beastly demons. The underworldly base of this cross has the usual hunting scenes common elsewhere.

The Celtic Cross at Moone is over 5 m (16½ ft) high and is set upon a tapering base surmounted by a pyramidal crown that in turn supports the shaft. This cross is believed to be the earliest that has a coherent scheme of decoration where episodes from the Old Testament and New Testament are arranged thematically. The basal stone is carved with various figures. The eastern front bears 12 figures, assumed to be the 12 apostles that were a popular theme for French Christians to carve on megaliths. Elsewhere on the basal stone are representations of those themes of the Perennial Philosophy that can be interpreted differently according to the beliefs of the beholder. Thus, the representation of the man amid the beasts, well known from Egyptian, Babylonian and Greek Paganism, becomes the Judaeo-Christian motif of Daniel in the Lions' Den. Just below the cross top on the eastern side, a panel in the shape of an Egyptian Diamond contains a figure that may be interpreted as the risen Christ. The centre of the cross does not have a crucifixion scene, but spirals. On the opposite, western side, there is a crucifixion scene, but again this is placed beneath the cross and not at its centre.

Made of granite quarried at Castledermot, the cross at Moone was lost for centuries, having been broken and the fragments buried. It was rediscovered shortly after the Potato Famine, when the local stonemason, Michael O'Shaughnessy, unearthed its base and head while collecting pieces of stone from the ruined abbey for new buildings. The cross-fragments were recovered, and the head was set up on the base. Later, during grave-digging, a part of the shaft was excavated. In 1893, three of O'Shaughnessy's sons reassembled the three parts, but with some of the shaft still missing. So it stands today.

At Kells in the county of Meath are four crosses that remain in various stages of integrity. They form the fourth group of Irish Celtic Crosses. Three stand within the church precincts, and the fourth stands in the middle of the road at the centre of the town as a market cross. One of the churchyard crosses is broken and incomplete, while another, perhaps the most interesting of the four crosses, is unfinished. This 'Unfinished Cross' was assembled in the nineteenth century from some cross-components that had for some reason been abandoned before finishing. Because of this fortunate accident of fate, we can see the way that the stonemason carved the basic form to allow the laying-out of interlace and figure patterns. The other three crosses were finished, and contain a wealth of figure sculpture of Biblical and other scenes that include some remarkable symbolism. The Broken Cross has a scene of the Baptism of Christ, in which the River Jordan is shown as a confluence of streams coming from two circular wells,

The Broken Cross has a scene of the Baptism of Christ, in which the River Jordan is shown as a confluence of streams coming from two circular wells, reflecting the Celtic veneration of sources of rivers.

reflecting the Celtic veneration of sources of rivers such as the Seine, Shannon and Severn. The South Cross at Kells also contains an image that is a clear continuation of Pagan tradition. At the centre of the wheel-head is an image of Christ in the posture of the Egyptian god Osiris, who was slain and resurrected like Jesus. The Osiris-Christ holds a cross and a blooming bough that alludes to the legendary golden bough and silver branch of Druidism. The market cross is notable for its scenes of the Celtic martial arts, including wrestling and quarter-staff fighting.

The fifth class of Irish high crosses is characterized by the now-destroyed Cross of Armagh, formerly at the headquarters of the archbishops of Ireland. Now only a few pieces remain, but its former glory is recorded in old engravings which show that the cross was covered with Biblical episodes arranged in a strictly logical order. The cross at Arboe in County Tyrone is the best surviving example of this rigorous arrangement.

The sixth group includes crosses at Clonmacnois, Monasterboice and Durrow. Clonmacnois in County Offaly preserves a fine collection of Celtic carvings. It is renowned for its grave-slabs, carved with Celtic crosses, names and invocations in ancient script. There are also a number of ancient crosses at Clonmacnois. A fragment of headless cross-shaft that exists to the north of the old church bears a carving of the horned god of the forest, Cernunnos, who in Brittany was worshipped as St Hoeirnin. Often, far from being destroyed by Christian priests, images of the old gods were maintained at the shrines where once they were the chief deities. St Fergus's cemetery on the island of Innishkeen in Upper Loch Erne still preserves the antlered stone head of a Celtic divinity. This Clonmacnois cross dates from around the year 800. The South Cross at Clonmacnois is a little more recent, dating from around 825. It is mostly carved with interlace and bosses, with a crucifixion on the westward side.

Considered to be one of the finest Celtic Crosses in Ireland is Flann's Cross. Named after King Flann, it is also called The Cross of the Scriptures. It stands to the west of the enclosure at Clonmacnois. A mutilated inscription at the bottom of the cross-shaft commemorates Flann, who died in the year 916, and Abbot Colman, who died in 921. Above the inscription is a carving of the king and abbot setting up a post, which may represent a cross. The centre of the wheel-cross has an image of Christ enthroned in the Osirian position. The ring of this cross is emphasized. Instead of the usual method of construction, in which the stonemasons made a cross and attached four arcs of stone to make the wheel, the designer of this cross emphasized the wheel in the form of a continuous stone ring linking four roundels. Thus, the centre cross with Christ in majesty is separated from the arms of the cross outside the ring. On top of the cross is a carving of a house-shrine.

At Monasterboice in County Louth are two more fine Celtic Crosses, both of which are intact and on their original sites. The West

Cross, which measures 6.7 m (22 ft) is the highest ancient cross remaining in Ireland. The cross-shaft is carved with panels that represent scenes from Biblical mythology. The wheel-head of the West Cross, which contains a number of bosses, is in a better state of preservation than the shaft or the house-shrine cap. It is likely that the cross was repaired in antiquity with new stone that replaced the original, for the depiction of the crucified Christ, whose head lolls to one side, is in the manner of later styles.

The other, more famous, cross at Monasterboice (illustrated on page 84) , is that of Muiredach, named after the Abbot who died in the year 922. He is commemorated by an inscription at the base of the shaft on the west side. The cross measures 5.5 m (18 ft), though some of the lower part of the shaft is missing now, the cross having been re-erected on its original pyramidal base. This cross is a remarkable synopsis of syncretic religion. Its east and west faces are sculpted with Biblical scenes, while the sides have spirals, bosses with interlace, and intertwining beasts. The outer part of the wheel-head is carved with bands of interlace between which are intertwining serpents. At the centre of the east face is an image of Christ, based on the iconography of the resurrected Egyptian god, Osiris. Christ is holding a cross and *Irminsul*-staff in the Osirian position, and on his head is an eagle that resembles the crown of Egyptian gods and pharaohs. On the left of Christ is the Great God Pan with his pipes, while on the right is a harp-playing figure, who is King David or Apollo. The tension between the emotional left side, and the rational right side is resolved in the figure of Christ, the perfect man.

The seventh and final grouping of high crosses arose in Ireland during the eleventh century, perhaps in County Clare, where a school of crossmakers operated from the late eleventh to the mid-twelfth centuries. There are six known crosses in this style at Kilfenora, three of which have sculpted figures. The Doorty Cross here has complex animal interlace. In comparison with the 'scriptural' high crosses, the figure sculpture of this school has been increased in size, the crucifixion is more prominent, interlace is reduced or absent and ring-heads, where present, are no longer pierced or drilled through. There are cross-fragments in this style in the churchyard at Killeany in the Aran Islands, but the most famous example stands at Dysert O'Dea. Although the pyramidal base of earlier crosses is retained, along with a pyramidal capstone, the mason created a cross-head without a ring, but with knobs in place of the customary holes. With a relatively large

OPPOSITE: Tomb-slabs with Celtic Crosses from Ireland. *Clockwise from top left:* tombstone of the smith Tuathal Saer, Clonmacnois, County Offaly; stone of Algidu, Durrow, Offaly; uninscribed cross-slab, Clonmacnois; slab of Mael Finnia, Clonmacnois.

Christ figure, the cross effectively became a crucifix. Beneath Christ, the customary scenes from Biblical episodes are no longer present; instead, a medieval bishop, complete with mitre and spiral-headed crozier, stands guard. Crosses of this period are relatively localized to the west and south midlands of Ireland. They are known from Cashel, Drumcliff, Inishcaltra, Mona Incha, Roscrea, Sligo and Tuam. There is only one exception, at Glendalough, in the east of Ireland.

SCOTTISH HIGH CROSSES

Outside Ireland, the Celtic Crosses on the holy island of Iona and at Kildalton on Islay in Strathclyde are closest in design to the Irish high crosses. The ninth-century cross in the churchyard at Kildalton is the most impressive surviving wheel-head Celtic Cross outside Ireland. Measuring 2.7 m (9 ft) in height, the whole cross was carved from one piece of stone. It has a few bosses and serpents, but these are subordinate to spirals, interlace and panels containing episodes from the Old Testament. According to a 1982 survey of Iona by experts from the Royal Commission on the Ancient and Historical Monuments of Scotland, St John's, St Martin's and St Oran's crosses were made during the second half of the eighth century. St Matthew's Cross, of which only a fragment still exists, dates from the late ninth or early tenth centuries. It has been suggested that St John's Cross was made originally without a wheel-head, and that, because it was weak, had the ring added later to strengthen it. Made of stone imported from Argyll, it had one of the widest spans of any cross known in the British Isles. Its original base now supports a replica.

Like St John's Cross and that at Kildalton, the Ionan cross of St Martin is a fine example of the 'boss style', carved with masterly skill. The arms of this cross have slots at the end which may have held metal or wooden pieces, perhaps for the suspension of garlands, ribbons or banners. The 'serpent stone' bosses on St Martin's Cross resemble those on the Dunfallandy cross-slab in Tayside, and the Irish high crosses at Ahenny and the South Cross at Clonmacnois. Although commentators have suggested that they are derived from metalworking, they and their metal counterparts resemble the rope knotwork used in sailing ships and practised today by canal-boat enthusiasts. The astonishing Celtic knotwork plug for the font in the church at Kilpeck in Hereford and Worcester is another parallel which is often overlooked. The creation of Celtic high crosses continued on Iona long after they had passed into

St Martin's Cross on the holy island of Iona is one of the finest still standing in the British Isles. *(Historic Scotland)*

The churchyard high cross at Kildalton, Islay, Scotland, of typical Irish form in the 'boss style', and standing on its original stepped base. *(Historic Scotland)*

the 'gothic' style elsewhere. Later high crosses, such as the fifteenth-century MacLean's Cross on Iona, are rather simple when compared with the scriptural crosses of Ireland and Islay. Later medieval high crosses, such as MacMillan's Cross at Kilmorie in Knapdale, retain the circular portion of the wheel-head but no longer have the wheel form. Instead, at Kilmorie, there is a crucifixion scene, and the lower part bears a sword flanked by simple interlace carving.

OPPOSITE: MacMillan's Cross at Kilmorie, Knapdale, Strathclyde. This fifteenth-century cross perpetuates the Celtic shape, but without a wheel or holes, as a crucifix. Interlace patterns are reduced, though the 'holu hill' base of the earlier Celtic Crosses is retained, maintaining the cosmic axis symbolism.

11

THE FALL AND RISE
OF THE CELTIC CROSS

The advent of the Gothic art style led to the end of the Celtic high cross. In prosperous places, more ornate architectural styles were favoured, and high crosses were superseded. In remote, poorer areas, such as the Highlands and Islands of Scotland, the Celtic high cross was simplified, eventually losing its main characteristics. However, although the ornate high crosses were no longer made, the tradition of Celtic interlace art did not die out, but was maintained throughout the middle ages by craftspeople in Ireland, parts of Wales and the west Highlands of Scotland. Appropriately, the holy island of Iona remained a significant centre of the tradition. The medieval sculptors who carved grave-slabs in the west Highlands re-interpreted the traditional interlace patterns once used on high crosses in combination with contemporary artistic styles. In Ireland and Wales, too, the knowledge of the art did not die out, but adapted itself according to the tastes of the time.

CONTINUITY AND DESTRUCTION

There are a number of surviving late medieval artefacts that demonstrate the continuation of traditional Celtic art. A notable Irish example is the fifteenth-century leather satchel made as a container for *The Book of Armagh*. Kept in Trinity College, Dublin, it is stamped with patterns that reflect the full repertoire of Celtic ribbonwork and animal interlaces. The famous ivory and metal Eglinton Casket (on show in the National Museum of Antiquities in Edinburgh), once thought to date from the first millennium, appears to be one of the finest products of the west Highlands in the early sixteenth century. The brass ring brooch from Tomintoul, Grampian, illustrated here, dates from the seventeenth century and contains wonderful four- and five-fold knot-work roundels. This so-called 'revival' demonstrates that the principles of Celtic interlace were understood and used by traditional craftspeople in Scotland well into the eighteenth century. It seems that the catastrophes of the Jacobite rebellions and the subsequent repression of Highland culture after 1746 led to the suspension of Celtic art in Scotland for a period, but not to its permanent suppression.

A seventeenth-century Scottish brass brooch from Tomintoul, Grampian, showing the continued understanding of Celtic interlace design which continued until the renewed interest in Celtic art in Queen Victoria's reign.

At the Reformation, places and things formerly revered by Roman Catholics as holy were condemned by the new Protestants as objects of superstition that should be destroyed. In those parts of the British Isles where staunch Protestants gained the ascendancy, most of the crosses were destroyed in the religious turmoil that marked the change from Catholicism. Puritan zealots believed it to be their religious duty to eliminate all 'idolatrous images' at which Catholic 'superstition' was practised. So, when they smashed and burnt the church's images of Christ, Our Lady and the saints, broke stained-glass windows and dug up altars, they also destroyed stone crosses both on church ground and at the wayside. An English law against witchcraft, passed in 1542, specifically mentions the latter practice, in the shape of certain people who had 'digged up and pulled down an infinite number of crosses within this realm, for despite of Christ, or for love of money'.

It was the Puritan destroyers, however, who by their activism had led the way in smashing churches. Because of their activities, those who believed treasure to lie beneath crosses could dig without fear of divine vengeance. However, the law did not recognize this, and condemned cross-destroyers as anti-Christian witches, or alternatively as people who believed the widespread story that treasure could be discovered beneath crosses. Because the Protestants wrecked so many churches and crosses without divine vengenace descending upon them, it became apparent to everyone that anyone could vandalize or loot a church or dig up a cross without fear of God's summary punishment. Then destruction could proceed without hindrance. In Scotland, the Edinburgh Parliament authorized the destruction of sacred places in 1581 with an act that stated: 'the Dregs of Idolatry yet remain in divers Parts of the Realm by using of Pilgrimage to some Chapels, Wells, Crosses, and such other Monuments of Idolatry, as also by observing the Festal days of the Saints sometime Named their Patrons in setting forth of Bon-Fires, singing of Carols within and about Kirks at certain Seasons of the Year.' This act to extirpate folk piety was the authorization by which many Scottish crosses were cast down and smashed. A thousand years of tradition was broken at a stroke.

So, outside Ireland and South Uist, which remained largely Catholic, the crosses were destroyed wholesale. As stone is a useful material, however, the pieces were not always thrown away, but re-used for other, profane, purposes. Fine crosses were broken up for their stone to be re-used as building material in houses, or as roadstone and gateposts. In some places, no use could be found for the crosses, so the fragments were buried or otherwise removed from sight. The scale of destruction was enormous. Before the Reformation, every churchyard had at least one cross; there were numerous wayside stopping-places marked by crosses, and every market-place had its market cross. Places of great sanctity had many crosses, and the oral tradition of Iona recalls that over 200 crosses from there and the islands nearby were tossed into the sea by fanatics.

THE RE-DISCOVERY
OF THE CELTIC HERITAGE

This wholesale destruction of sacred artefacts had an effect on art styles. After the Puritan iconoclasm, Celtic interlace was no longer seen as an everyday part of life by all those who passed the local cross. It became a misty memory, whose nature was misunderstood and unrecognized. Thus, in learned circles, most understanding of the principles of Celtic art was lost, though in certain craft circles the knowledge was maintained among initiates. Also, especially in Ireland, knowledge of other esoteric Celtic traditions was maintained by local bards, wise women and cunning men. Knowledge and use of the ogham script continued among the people, being used occasionally on tombstones until the present day. In the nineteenth century at Kinsale in County Cork lived a man named Collins who had a poem about the zodiac painted on his walking-stick in white ogham characters. His cart also bore his name in ogham, and he was prosecuted for not writing it in the Roman alphabet.

Even where Celtic art was not completely ignored, learned artists from the academies contented themselves with copying earlier examples as instances of ancient barbarism rather than high art with a contemporary value. Unfortunately, because they did not take care to work according to the proper principles, what they produced was of inferior quality, and often broke the simplest rules, such as those for constructing basic interlace patterns. Even those artists who worked with antiquaries to record the remains of ancient Celtic art often drew impressions of what they saw, rather than accurate detail. Camden's *Britannia*, the first great attempt to document British antiquities, contains illustrations that were insufficiently accurate

Scottish national romanticism, promoted by Sir Walter Scott … led to the revival of highland dress and the resumption of production of Celtic jewellery, based on surviving examples.

for later scientific archaeologists. However, it is only through the prodigious work of these early antiquaries that we know anything about many ancient crosses and other monuments. Another stalwart recorder of ancient monuments was the Oswestry scholar Edward Lhuyd (1660–1709), sometime keeper of the Ashmolean Museum in Oxford, who wrote about many Welsh antiquities that subsequently have been lost or destroyed.

It was not in Wales, however, that the fortunes of Celtic art first took a turn for the better, but in Scotland and Ireland. Scottish national romanticism, promoted by Sir Walter Scott and given considerable impetus by George IV's visit to Edinburgh in 1822, led to the revival of highland dress and the resumption of production of Celtic jewellery, based on surviving examples. Writing in *The British Architect* in 1875,

Derived from the Celtic Cross is the typical medieval cross of which this example stands in the churchyard at Cricklade, Wiltshire, England. *(Nigel Pennick)*

notable Neo-Gothic architect William Burges recognized Scott's seminal role, stating that '... the real restorer of medieval art was Sir Walter Scott'. After Scott's impetus, the restored tradition was reinforced later by Queen Victoria's patronage, which ultimately resulted in a return to the manufacture of Celtic Crosses in stone, mainly as graveyard memorials. Commentators on Celtic art often condemn this period as being a conscious revival that has no artistic or spiritual value. However, this attitude is often conditioned by the political theory that tradition has no place in the modern world. Nineteenth-century Celtic Crosses stand as authentic products of the Celtic spirit, however removed some of the individual pieces may be from the traditional current.

The general revival in Christian art in the United Kingdom under Queen Victoria, which at that time included the whole of Ireland, provided the impetus for proper study of ancient ecclesiastical art. Of course, the Celtic Cross was recognized then as one of the most notable instances of early Christian art in the British Isles. An interest in crosses in general was expressed by the publication in 1875 of Alfred Rimmer's *The Ancient Stone Crosses of England* (Virtue and Co.) Again, in this book, because of a lack of understanding of the principles, the illustration of Celtic interlace and key-patterns was poor, as in an engraving of the Nevern cross, which completely fails to depict the ornament correctly. However, Rimmer did express the general feeling of loss; that the sacred landscape had been destroyed wantonly by Puritan vandalism. 'Could road-side crosses have remained to the present day', wrote Rimmer, 'they would have been cherished objects in almost every village in England.'

Because of the dedicated work of antiquaries over the years, gradually a general awareness grew that the past mattered. Then, those old stone crosses that had been abandoned and used as bridges over streams, as building blocks or as gateposts to fields were located and removed to museums. In 1892, the antiquary Archdeacon Griffiths of Carmarthen donated an early Christian monument to the Cardiff Free Library and Museum. The process then began of taking away stone crosses from their original sites and displaying them in national museums in London, Cardiff, Edinburgh and Dublin. However, there was an alternative to the wholesale removal of monuments from their proper location. In the 1860s, the London firm of Brucciani and Company was established as the most able producer of plaster casts of antique monuments. The non-destructive technique used by Brucciani involved covering the stones with gelatine sheet and materials through which moisture could not penetrate. Then the clay and plaster used for the process of casting did not come into contact with the valuable carvings, yet reproduced them faithfully. This technique was used with ancient sculptures from Greece and Rome, and substantial collections of them still exist, most notably at the Museum of Classical Archaeology at Cambridge.

During the 1890s, a collection of Welsh crosses was begun by the curator of the Cardiff Free Library and Museum, which served as the basis for the present collection of crosses in the National Museum of

Wales. In 1894, using Brucciani's technique, a programme was set up to make and collect casts of ancient stones, beginning with the famous crosses and slabs from Margam and Bridgend. W. Clarke of Llandaff took over the task from Brucciani in 1900, and continued with the programme of making casts of all known stones. Being from Wales, Clarke's brief was expanded to look for any 'as yet undiscovered or forgotten', and, gradually, as in other parts of the British Isles, a comprehensive knowledge was built up. Casts of crosses from other parts of the British Isles were made at the same time, and some of these replicas can be seen in the Victoria and Albert Museum in London and the National Museum of Ireland in Dublin. Ironically, subsequent degradation of the real stones as the result of air pollution means that many of these replicas now show more detail than the originals.

Towards the end of the nineteenth century, antiquaries and archaeologists began to make systematic studies of the Celtic Crosses of their respective localities. In his *Old Cornish Crosses*, published in 1896, A. G. Langdon recorded 360 examples from that county alone, which made Rimmer's earlier estimate of 5,000 crosses in England appear rather conservative. The antiquary J. Romilly Allen (1847–1907) also took an academic approach to Celtic monuments, recording them accurately with measured drawings. It was Romilly Allen who laid the foundations for the current resurgence of Celtic art. His book, *The Early Christian Monuments of Scotland* (The Pinkfoot Press), published at Edinburgh in 1903, was followed by works on Wales and *Celtic Culture in Pagan and Pre-Christian Times* (1904). The results of the new science of archaeology were significant in the restoration of Celtic art that we see today. Nineteenth-century Romantic artists like William Hole integrated all sorts of Celtic archaeological artefacts from different places and periods into their historic paintings. Yet, despite their historical inaccuracy, there is no dissonance. Such paintings work as art, attesting to the underlying spirit of Celtic tradition.

At this time, as the result of a renewed interest in vernacular tradition, Celtic art assumed an important part in the repertoire of the Arts-and-Crafts movement. Based upon indigenous principles, it took traditional design elements and reinterpreted them in a modern form. Located at Compton, near Guildford in Surrey, the Watts Mortuary Chapel is one of the most remarkable Celtic Arts-and-Crafts buildings ever erected. Designed by Mary Fraser-Tytler Watts, wife of the eminent Victorian painter George Frederick Watts, it incorporates Celtic Crosses unlike any seen before, yet completely within the tradition.

The fine nineteenth-century Celtic Cross that marks the grave of the Welsh bard Tegid, co-translator of the *Mabinogion*, in the churchyard of St Brynach's, Nevern, Dyfed, Wales. *(Nigel Pennick)*

Each and every part of Mary Watts's chapel contains a symbolic meaning, reflecting her saying 'All creation is the garment of God'. Constructed of brick and terracotta, it is a masterly design of such stunning originality that makes it all the more regrettable that she spent her life in the shadow of 'England's Michelangelo' rather than practising in her own right as an architect. In keeping with the spiritual ethos of the Arts-and-Crafts movement, that local materials and techniques should be used as far as possible, she set up a pottery using local clay to make the terracotta panels, roundels and other decorative elements of the chapel. This pottery, which continued to produce wares until the 1950s, also made terracotta tombstones of various designs of Celtic Crosses, many of which can be seen in the graveyard in which the chapel is set. The chapel's symbolic decoration includes a number of roundels that progressively denote spiritual evolution in addition to the Celtic Cross illustrated here. Like ancient Celtic Crosses, the Watts chapel is truly part of the land, for it is made of materials won from the local earth, related perfectly to its location in the landscape.

On the Isle of Man, the Arts-and-Crafts architect Baillie Scott used the Celtic Cross in the ornament of some of his houses. For example, in Onchan, he built the houses Breaside and Leafield, and ornamented them with wheel-crosses made of pebbles standing proud of the cement rendering of the external walls. At Glen Falcon, built three years later in 1900, he made a copper fireplace-surround with a repoussé pattern of an eight-fold cross in Manx tradition. Ornamental elements from Celtic Crosses were popularized by the Manx designer Archibald Knox in his metalwork for Liberty and Company. In Ireland the Arts-and-Crafts-inspired Dun Emer Guild, founded by Evelyn Gleeson in 1902, produced textiles and carpets that used Celtic Cross interlace and tesselation patterns. Later, the foundation of the Irish Free State in 1921 gave impetus to the promotion of Celtic art as a national style. It has held its position since then.

However, Ireland's troubles also led to one of the worst losses of ancient Celtic manuscripts. This took place in June 1922 during the

Mary Watts's Celtic Cross design and altar cross for the Watts Mortuary Chapel at Compton, Surrey, England.

Irish Civil War, when the Four Courts in Dublin, held by Republican soldiers, was shelled by Free State artillery. The building, used by the Irish Republican Army as a munitions store, received a direct hit from a shell and exploded catastrophically. The Irish National Archive, held in the building and containing many priceless documents, was totally destroyed in one blow. After the victory of the Free State faction, however, Celtic monuments were erected to those who fell in the war. In the United Kingdom, too, to commemorate 'The Great War for Civilization', the Celtic Cross was adopted as the model for many of the numerous war memorials that were erected in almost every village to honour those who had died in the conflict. Wherever possible, the new British war memorials were erected at places where crosses had stood in former times. Thus, stone crosses were restored to the British landscape as new representatives of the 'cherished objects' whose loss Rimmer had lamented 50 years earlier.

In the 1920s, interest in Celtic artwork continued. In 1922, the English fantasy artist Sidney Sime designed a cover for the libretto of Josef Holbrooke's opera, *Bronwen*. It showed the hero and heroine standing beneath a Pictish-type cross-slab with interlace panels in the

Smaller examples of tombstones can also be interesting instances of more recent Celtic Crosses. An early twentieth-century example stands over the grave of Cecil Bendall, Professor of Sanskrit at Cambridge University, in St Giles's Cemetery, Cambridge, England. *(Nigel Pennick)*

form of a swastika. Of course, before the 1930s, that ancient sign had none of the bad connotations later attached to it by the Nazis. As an ancient symbol for lightning, it appears on ancient slabs like the Craignarget Stone, and occasionally upon graveyard memorials like Professor Cecil Bendall's Celtic Cross in Cambridge, which refers to his Hindu connections. Following the work of earlier antiquaries, especially Romilly Allen, from the 1920s, the Scottish artist George Bain investigated actual examples of Celtic art from Pictish stones and Celtic manuscripts, and, by analysis, expanded on Romilly Allen's re-discoveries. George Bain's main intention was to bring Celtic art back into the repertoire of contemporary artists, craftspeople and designers. His master-work, *Celtic Art: The Methods of Construction* (McLellan), first published in 1951, which contains his analysis, of the principles underlying Celtic art, has become the standard work on

Celtic art. As Bain intended, the book became the greatest influence on contemporary Celtic artists, and remains so today.

Through the work of Romilly Allen, George Bain and his son Iain, and the Irish artist John G. Merne, the principles of Celtic art are understood once more, and there has been a renaissance of Celtic art in every field except, paradoxically, that of making stone crosses. The Celtic artists Jim Fitzpatrick, Courtney Davis, David James and Simon Rouse are among the most notable contemporary exponents of the style in book illustrations, posters and paintings, often with a spiritual content. Fantasy artists, illustrating the works of J. R. R. Tolkien and his imitators, have taken to Celtic art as the authentic reflection of the elder times in northern Europe.

Similarly, with a recognition of ancestral tradition, contemporary jewellers are now making Celtic Crosses of precious metals as pendants to wear around the neck, and small replicas of Celtic Crosses are available as ornaments. Since the 1980s, elements of Celtic art have become a significant current

Fantasy artists, illustrating the works of J.R.R. Tolkien and his imitators, have taken to Celtic art as the authentic reflection of the elder times in northern Europe.

in the repertoire of the tattooist. Celtic Crosses, interlace and stylized animal patterns adorn the human body. This art is worldwide. Among the most notable contemporary tattooists putting Celtic Crosses on people are Darren Rosa and Jonathan Shaw of New York, Geoff Wilson of Lillydale, Australia, and 'Crazy Greg' of Heidelberg, Germany. Their work is in some way a contemporary restoration of the body art of the ancient Picts and Copts.

In 1996, the continuing awareness of the Celtic Cross was evidenced by the British Royal Mint issuing of a £1 coin, designed by Norman Sillman. Its reverse ('tails') side bears a Celtic Cross, representative of Northern Ireland. However, a revival of making new, full-sized, coloured Celtic Crosses is still awaited. All of the appropriate knowledge and skills exist among contemporary practitioners of Celtic art, and this is ample evidence that the Celtic tradition, already 2,700 years old, will continue to flourish in the foreseeable future.

GAZETTEER

In the gazetteer, numbers following the place names are Ordnance Survey grid references.

There are a large number of crosses and related stones remaining in the Celtic realms. It is not possible to list them all, nor are all of them accessible. Also, like everything in the landscape, crosses are subject to destruction, either through accident, neglect or unthinking development, like road-widening. So to visit the less famous examples may be either an adventure or a disappointment. Nevertheless, when we visit a Celtic Cross we should do it with reverence, not in an offhand manner as just the next sight to 'do' on a jaded tourist trail. Crosses should be treated with respect, and we should always bear in mind that each Celtic Cross is sacred, bearing witness to the universal human recognition of the divine powers that lie beyond human understanding.

BRITTANY

Bazoges-la-Pérouse, Ile-et-Vilaine. La Pierre Longue (or La Pierre de Lande-Ros) stands near a stream between Bazoges and Noyal, 2 km (1 mile) from the crossroads of Trois-Croix. It is a megalith whose top has been carved into a Christian cross.

Brigognan-Plage, Finistère. The Men Marz at the Terre-de-Point 1 km (½ mile) to the north-northwest of Brigognan-Plage is known as a miracle stone where St Pol de Leon stopped the encroachment of the sea. It bears a small cross on its summit.

Carnac-Ville, Carnac. La Pierre Chaude (or Cruz-Moquen) is a megalithic tomb upon which stands a tall stone cross.

Hameau de Rungleo, Finistère. Near Daoulas (45 km/28 miles southwest of Morlais, 18 km/11 miles eastsoutheast of Brest) is the Croix des Douze Apôtres, a megalith re-dedicated as a Christian monument in the late medieval period. The figures resemble those on the base of the cross at Moone, County Kildare, Ireland.

Kerégard-Vraz, Plumeur, Finistère. (23 km/14 miles southwest of Quimper, 6 km/3½ miles west of Pont l'Abbé.) Narrow, rounded, granite megalith cross.

Lanrivoaré, Finistère. Close to the church is 'The Moaning-Place', eight megalithic boulders, with a stone cross, that mark, it is said, a massacre in the fifth century, clearly a place of ancestral memory.

Penvern, Côte-du-Nord. (9 km/5½ miles northwest of Lannion, 3 km/2 miles northnortheast of Trébeurden.) The cross of St Duzec, 8.1 m (26½ ft) high, is a megalith that was rededicated as a Christian monument in 1674. It bears carvings of the instruments of the passion, and has a cross bearing the crucified Christ on top. Also near Penvern, near Keralies, is one of St Samson's menhirs, next to a chapel constructed between 1575 and 1631.

Plévenon, Côte-du-Nord. At Cap Fréhel, 3 km (2 miles) northeast of Plévenon, is L'Aiguille de Gargantua, a megalith re-fashioned as a shaft surmounted by a cross.

St Samson-sur-Rance, La Tremblais, Côte-du-Nord. 5 km (3 miles) northeast of Dinan in the village of St Samson close to the road to La Quinardais is another of St Samson's stones with finely incised bands of rectangles with cup-marks.

GREAT BRITAIN

Aberlemno, Tayside (NO 5255). Alongside the B9134 road in Aberlemno are three Pictish 'symbol stones', while the churchyard to the east of this road contains the misleadingly named 'Aberlemno Stone', an eighth-century stone with an incised cross accompanied by beasts and hunting scenes.

Babingley, Norfolk (TF 6726). The stump of a cross near the crossroads, Boteler's Cross, could be the site of the first Christian settlement in East Anglia, founded by St Felix of Burgundy in the seventh century.

Bangor, Gwynedd (SH 5872). The Museum of Welsh Antiquities at Bangor contains some early Celtic cross-slabs.

Beverley, Humberside (TA 0339). Three of the four crosses that marked the boundary of the sanctuary of Beverley Minster can be seen: at Walkington (TA 0037), the cross is a stump in the hedge at the beginning of the village; Stump Cross at Killingwoldgraves (TA 0039); and next to the Beverley-to-Hessle road at Bentley (TA 0236).

Borthwick Mains, Borders (NI 4314). A Pictish symbol stone, in the private garden of a farm 6.4 km (4 miles) west of Hawick, once stood in the River Teviot. Carved on the stone is a fish whose tail is said to be a marker of the level of water at which it was safe to ford the river.

Brechin, Tayside (NO 5960). Preserved in the cathedral is a fragment of cross that has an image of the Madonna and Child in a circular medallion at the centre of the cross-head. There is also the fine Celtic cross-slab called the Aldbar Stone, after its finding-place at Aldbar Castle. The front is carved with interlace while the rear has animals, humans and implements.

Brecon, Powys (SO 0428). Brecknock Museum on Captain's Walk in Brecon has a collection of stone stelae and crosses, including the Neuadd Siarman cross from Llanynys.

Bridell, Dyfed (SN 1742). In the churchyard stands a pointed megalith inscribed with an ogham text, which, translated, reads 'Nettasagrus, son of the descendant of Brecus'. On one side is an equal-armed cross within a circle, added in the ninth century.

Carew, Dyfed (SN 0403). Beside the A4075 road, in the wall close to the castle entrance, is an eleventh-century cross, commemorating King Maredudd ap Edwin, who ruled Deheubarth (the kingdom of South-West Wales) from 1033 until 1035.

Cardinham, Cornwall (SX 1269). The church has a fine Celtic Cross of typically Cornish tradition.

Carmarthen Museum, Old Bishop's Palace, Abergwili, Carmarthen, Dyfed (SN 4120). This museum has a collection of early Christian monuments, including the stone of Voteporix Protector.

Carnoustie, Tayside Region (NO 5137). In the grounds of Panmure House, 6.5 km (4 miles) north of Carnoustie, stands the Camus Cross or Jesus Stone, a late Celtic Cross without a wheel-head.

Chapel of Garioch, Grampian Region (NJ 7124). A 3.6-m (12-ft) high cross-shaft called 'The Maiden Stone' stands just outside the village.

Clackmannan, Central Region (NS 9191). In the churchyard is the phallic megalith that was used in the ceremony of inauguration by Pictish rulers. Next to it is a stepped perron.

Compton, Surrey (SU 9547). The Watts Mortuary Chapel at Compton is a remarkable symbolic building in Celtic Arts-and-Crafts style, designed by the Scottish artist Mary Fraser-Tytler Watts, constructed in 1896. Terracotta Celtic Cross motifs are used in the building and as tombstones in the graveyard.

Cringleford, Norfolk (TG 1905). Parts of a 'runic cross', discovered during rebuilding in 1898, are on the wall behind the font.

Dartmoor, Devon. The sacred stopping-places on the monastic trackway between Tavistock (SX 4774) and Buckfast (SX 7367) are marked by the following crosses: Tavistock Abbey – Green Lane Cross – Pixies' Cross – Warren's Cross – Huckworthy Cross – Walkhampton Church House Cross – Yannandon Cross – Lower Lowery Cross – Lowery Cross – Lether Tor Bridge – Clazywell Cross – Newley-combe Cross – Siward's Cross – Nun's Cross – Goldsmith's Cross – Childe's Tomb Cross – Mount Misery Cross – West Ter Hill Cross – East Ter Hill Cross – Skaur Ford Cross – Horse Ford Cross – Horn's Cross – Two Thorns Cross – Play Cross – Hawson Cross – Buckfast Abbey.

Dunfallandy, Tayside (NN 9456). Here is a Pictish cross-slab which shows the boss-style at its most prominent, and some of the finest beast-carvings on a Celtic Cross.

Dunning, southwest of Perth, Tayside (NO 0114). On the road to Milhaugh, west of Dunning, is a perron-cross that stands upon a rough stepped-stone base. It is respected as the memorial to Maggie Wall, who was burnt there as a witch in 1657.

Dunkeld, Tayside (NO 0242). Preserved in the cathedral is the Apostles' Stone, a piece of cross-shaft with carvings of 12 figures, stylistically related to many 'Twelve Apostles' Stones' elsewhere.

Dupplin, near Forteviot, Tayside (NO 0518). An Irish-influenced free-standing cross is here.

Ewenni Priory Church, Glamorgan (SS 9177). This church has a number of interesting cross-slabs.

Forres, Grampian (NJ 0358). The tenth-century Sueno's Stone, over 6 m (20 ft) high, is carved with contemporary scenes of hunting and battle.

Fowey, Cornwall (SX 1152). On the A3082 near Fowey is the Tristan Stone, a pedestal bearing a sixth-century stone with an inscription commemorating Drustanus, perhaps the Arthurian Tristan or Tristram. Before 1971, the stone stood at the Four Turnings crossroads near Menabilly.

Fowlis Wester, Tayside region (NN 9223). The 'sculptured stone' of Foulis Wester is a fine cross-slab which depicts a free-standing wheel-head cross flanked by seated figures. The cross is ornamented with spirals, interlace and key-patterns.

Govan, Strathclyde (NS 5565). The old Govan church contains a collection of ancient Celtic Crosses and other worked stones.

Great Ashfield, Suffolk (TL 9968). A wheel-head cross stands in the grounds of Ashfield House. In former times, it was used as a bridge over the stream at the churchyard entrance.

Hackness, North Yorkshire (SE 9690). A fragment of eighth-century cross is kept in the church, which is the site of an Anglo-Saxon nunnery. Carved with interlace, it bears a multiple inscription in standard runes, the cryptic runes known as *hahal-runa*, and ogham.

Hilton, Cambridgeshire (TL 2966). The parish church has a small but ancient Celtic Cross attached to the west wall.

Hoxne, Suffolk (TM 1876). In a field close to Hoxne is a cross on steps, erected in 1870 to commemorate the reputed execution of King Edmund of East Anglia on a tree that stood at this place until 1848.

Iona, Inner Hebrides, Strathclyde (NM 2726). The old Gaelic name for Iona is Innis na Druineach (The Isle of the Druids). St Columba founded St Mary's Abbey there in 563, and by the Reformation there were over 350 Celtic Crosses on the island. At the Reformation, Protestants threw over 200 of them into the sea, so now only the fifteenth-century Maclean's Cross and the tenth-century St Martin's Cross remain standing.

Kedington, Suffolk (TL 7047). On the gable at the east end of the church is the uppermost part of an ancient wheel-head cross, which was placed there after it was excavated from beneath the chancel floor.

Keills, Strathclyde (NR 6980). The old chapel here contains several Celtic crosses and other carved stones.

Kenidjack, Cornwall (SW 3631 and SW 3645). Two cross-pillars, from Trevorian in Sennen Parish, stand in the grounds of Boscean Hotel.

Kildalton, Islay (NR 4550). The tenth-century wheel-headed Celtic Cross in Kildalton churchyard is the finest in Scotland.

Kilmory, Knap, Strathclyde (NR 7075). At Kilmory is an old chapel containing Celtic Crosses and other Celtic carvings.

Lanherne, St Mawgan, Cornwall (SX 2368). A notable Cornish cross stands here.

Laugharne, Dyfed (SN 3011). A notable Celtic Cross is preserved at the church.

Littleton Drew, Wiltshire (ST 8280). Two cross-fragments at the church may be the remains of one of the crosses erected to mark a stopping-place of St Aldhelm's funeral procession from Doulting to Malmesbury.

Llandewibrefi, Dyfed (SN 6755). The parish church has a fine cross.

Llandough, South Glamorgan (SS 9972). The churchyard of St Dochdwy contains a unique four-section pillar cross, 'The Stone of Irbic'. It has a 'holy mountain' base with a carving of a horseman and the bust of a man.

Llangammarch, Powys (SN 9347). Over the door of the church porch is a fragment of a ninth- or tenth-century sunwheel-cross, with a human figure and a spiral below, perhaps a serpent.

Llan-gan, West Glamorgan (SS 9678). A ninth- or tenth-century disc-headed sandstone cross bearing a figure of Christ stands in the churchyard.

Llangollen, Clwyd (SJ 2044). A stone cross-shaft known as 'The Pillar of Eliseg' is in a railing enclosure close to the Cistercian Abbey of Valle Crucis. It contains a geneology of Eliseg, a ninth-century worthy.

Llantwit Major, South Glamorgan (SS 9678). In the church is a rather poorly presented collection of ancient Celtic Crosses, including that of Hywel ap Rhys, king of Glywysing, who died in 886, and a remarkable serpent's head. The churchyard contains a fine perron, and there is a 'death road' called Burial Lane that leads to the churchyard.

Lonan, near Ballamenaugh, Isle of Man (SC 4279). This has a notable cross-slab.

Ludgvan, Cornwall (SW 5033). The churchyard contains a cross-slab and two larger ancient standing crosses.

Margam Stones Museum, The Old School House, Margam, West Glamorgan (SS 7887). A valuable collection of ancient Celtic Crosses and slabs from the early days of the Christian religion in Wales. It includes the sixth-century Bodvocus stone. In the ninth and tenth centuries, there was a school of cross-sculptors at Margam, and the Conbelin wheel-head cross displayed here is a fine example of their work.

Maughold, Isle of Man (SC 4991). The churchyard has a collection of Celtic Crosses and stones.

Meigle, Alyth, Tayside (NO 2844). An important collection of Pictish cross-slabs is displayed here.

Merthyr Mawr, Mid Glamorgan (SS 8877). Here there is a panelled cross with a broken interlaced head, a characteristic example of the style.

Methwold, Norfolk (TL 7394). At Cross Hill is an ancient stone that once held a wooden cross-shaft, now lost.

Mold (Yr Wyddgrug), Clwyd (SL 2363). In Maesgarmon Field, off the Gwernaffield Road, stands the 'Alleluia Stone', erected by Nehemiah Griffith in 1736 to commemorate the victory of Bishop Germanus's army over Saxon and Pictish forces in 429 CE.

Montrose, Tayside Region (NO 7157). Preserved in the museum at Montrose is the damaged Pictish cross-slab from Farnell, which has a famous image of the Tree of Life with Adam and Eve, two serpents and a cross. Also in the museum is a cross-slab from Inchbrayock with spirals and key-patterns.

Mylor, Cornwall (SW 8235). The churchyard contains the tallest cross in Cornwall, with solar carvings.

Nanquidno, Cornwall (SW 3629). A wheel-head cross, with a cross and bosses in relief, marks a stopping-place on the track to Nanquidno Farm.

Nevern, Dyfed (SN 0839). The churchyard contains a phallic stone and a Celtic Cross, dating from the tenth or eleventh centuries. Inside the church are ancient cross- and ogham-stones. At the end of the churchyard is the nineteenth-century Celtic Cross marking the grave of the bard Tegid, the Reverend John Jones, located at the only place in the churchyard from which one can see St Brynach's holy mountain, Carn Ingli.

Nigg, Highland (NH 8071). In the old parish church is the broken cross-slab notable for its fine bosses, carved with interlace and six-fold spirals.

Old Town, St Mary's, Isles of Scilly (SV 9210). A granite cross formerly at High Cross Lane, Salakee, is mounted on the gable end of St Mary's Church at Old Town.

Paul, Cornwall (SW 4627). On the churchyard wall is a four-hole wheel-head with a clothed Christ figure. Nearby is a round-headed cross, the shaft of which has carved crosses.

Penally, Dyfed (SS 1199). The church contains a whole wheel-head cross with interlace and scroll patterns, with some original red colour remaining, and a second fragment with opposed animals and interlace.

Pendrea, Cornwall (SW 4025). A round-headed cross with a cross on one side and Christ on the other stands by the road from Buryan to Land's End.

Penmon, Anglesey (SH 6380). The Priory Church contains two notable Celtic Crosses.

Penrith, Cumbria (NY 5130). In St Andrew's churchyard are cross-fragments that mark 'The Giant's Grave', said to be the grave of the giant Isir, who resided in a nearby cave.

Penzance, Cornwall (SW 4730). Outside the Penlee Museum, Morrab Road, Penzance, is preserved a notable tenth-century wheel-head cross which once stood at another site, serving as a market cross. Its shaft is divided into panels, some of which bear peck-marks that may have held painted cement or plaster in former times. There are the remains of an inscription, interpreted as *Regis Ricati Crux*, 'The cross of King Ricatus'.

Perranporth, Cornwall (SW 7756). A cross mentioned in a charter of the year 960 stands close to the celebrated 'lost church'.

Rosemorran, Cornwall (SW 4732). In the hedge at the back of the farmyard is a round-headed cross, which has Christ on one side and a cross on the other.

Rossie Priory, Tayside (NO 2930). The characteristic Pictish 'page in stone'.

Rudston, Yorkshire (TA 0967). At Rudston Church is a millstone grit pillar which is the largest megalith in a British churchyard.

St Buryan, Cornwall. Close to St Buryan are a number of interesting crosses. At Boskenna (SW 4324) on the B3315 to the southeast of St Buryan, is a broken, wheel-head cross set into a cider-press stone. Another is located to the north of it at Vellansagia (SW 4325), and to the northwest of St Buryan (SW 3927), next to a fine milestone, is Crows-an-Wra, 'The Cross of the Witch', after which the nearby hamlet is named.

St Cleer, north of Liskeard, Cornwall (SX 2468). Near the fifteenth-century house of St Cleer's Well is a Latin cross, while on the road to Redgate about 1.5 km (1 mile) away is the fragment of a tenth-century inscribed stone that recalls the memory of Doniert, King of Cornwall, who drowned in the River Fowey in 875.

St David's, Dyfed (SM 7525). The chapel containing the relics of St David has an altar composed of a number of ancient Celtic cross-slabs and test-pieces.

St Dogmaels, Dyfed (SN 4715). In the abbey ruins is a lapidarium that contains many interesting old stones, including several cross-slabs, one of which is humanoid.

St Just, Cornwall (SW 3631). St Helen's Chapel at Cape Cornwall has an ancient cross erected on a gable end.

St Michael's Mount, Cornwall (SW 5129). This holy mountain of the Sun contains four crosses that mark sacred stopping-places around the former monastery.

St Vigeans, Tayside (NO 6342). At St Vigeans is an important collection of Pictish cross-slabs, one of which (The Drosten Stone, St Vigeans I) has a *sheela-na-gig*. On the back of this stone is the earliest known representation of a crossbowman.

Sancreed, southeast of St Just, Cornwall (SW 4129). Sancreed churchyard possesses two notable wheel-head monolithic crosses, one of which bears an image of the Christ and the inscription *Runho*, perhaps the crossmaster's name.

Southrepps, Norfolk (TG 2636). The broken shaft of an Anglian cross stands near the crossroads outside the village.

Temple, Cornwall (TX 5574). A number of ancient cross-incised stones and stone crosses are built into the wall of this church.

Terrington St John, Norfolk (TF 5415). The vicarage garden contains one of the crosses known as 'Hickathrift's Candlesticks'. It was named after the solar giant of the Norfolk marshland, and perhaps a one-time god of the Celtic Iceni tribe, Tom Hickathrift.

Thurso, Highland region (ND 1168). Thurso Museum has a fine collection of Pictish stones, among them the eighth-century Ulbser and Skinner Stones, with crosses and beasts.

Tilney All Saints, Norfolk (TF 5618). Two crosses in the churchyard, called 'Tom Hichathrift's Candlesticks', once marked the reputed grave of this Norfolk hero-giant.

Towton, North Yorkshire (SE 4839). Next to the B1217 Towton Lane is Lord Dacre's Cross, erected to commemorate the battle fought there on Palm Sunday, 1461, in which 36,000 died.

Trelleck, Gwent (SO 5005). Outside the church is a stone cross, standing on a stepped 'world mountain' base, erected by an early medieval king of this part of Wales.

Walsingham, Norfolk (TF 9336). Some of the stopping-places of pilgrim routes to Walsingham, Britain's primary Marian shrine, were marked by crosses, some of which still remain: e.g. at Binham (TG 9839); Caston (TG 9697); Gresham (TG 1838); Hemsby (TG 4917); and Weeting (TG 7739).

Whissonsett, Suffolk (TF 9123). The church contains the remains of a stone cross with interlace.

Whitecross, Cornwall (SW 5234). Beside the main A30 road in Ludgvan parish stands a cross-head supported by two stone blocks. It is whitewashed annually in a ceremony.

Whitford, Clwyd (SJ 1477). Maen Achwyfan, 'The Stone of Lamentations' is a late tenth-century wheel-head cross-slab with designs related to Northumbrian cross-decoration, including spirals and interlace.

Whithorn, Galloway (NX 4440). The museum at Whithorn contains a collection of crosses.

IRELAND

Ahenny, Kilkenny (X 2413). At the monastic settlement of Kilclispeen are two eighth-century high crosses. The North Cross, which is damaged, is a remarkable sunwheel with five prominent bosses, a finely carved wheel and a conical capstone.

Ardboe, Tyrone (H 2937). The high cross with Biblical figures is reputed to be the finest in the north of Ireland.

Boa Island, Lower Lough Erne, Fermanagh (G 2136). At the west end of the island, in the cemetery of Caldragh, stand a Pagan Janiform stone figure and another image called 'The Lusty Man'. Also, lined up in a roofless twelfth-century church, is a collection of seven stone figures dating from around 900. They include a *sheela-na-gig*, a seated man holding a book, and an ecclesiastical figure with crozier and bell.

Cardonagh, Inishowen, Donegal (C 2444). West of Cardonagh is the Donagh Cross or St Patrick's Cross. It is said to be the oldest low-relief cross still standing in Ireland.

Castledermot, Kildare (S 2818). Castledermot, named after St Diarmuid, the founder (*c.* 800), has two interesting high crosses, the north of which has particularly fine spiral carvings on its 'holy mountain' base.

Clones, Monaghan (N 2532). There is a Celtic Cross in the centre of the town of Clones.

Clonmacnois, Offaly (N 2023). This is one of the most important Celtic Church foundations in Ireland, founded by St Ciarán in 548 on royal ground given by King Diarmid. It has several fine Celtic high crosses and a remarkable collection of Celtic grave-slabs with crosses, interlace and inscriptions.

Cooley, Donegal (N 2544). In the cemetery of Cooley, 3 km (2 miles) north of Moville, the reputed burial place of St Finian, are two notable crosses.

Devenish, Fermanagh (H 2234). Daimh Inish, the Island of Oxen, in Lower Lough Erne, the holy island of St Molaise, has an unusual cross, as well as a monastic museum.

Durrow, south of Kilbeggan, Offaly (N 2323). Northeast of Durrow Abbey is a tenth-century high cross and the holy well of St Columba.

Dysert O'Dea (R 1218). The high cross here has interlace and zoomorphic figures, and a stone representing St Tola, the eighth-century founder.

Fahan, Buncrana, Donegal (C 2343). 7 km (4½ miles) south of Buncrana, at Fahan, is St Mura's Cross, a stone with remarkable interlace and human figures. Close by is another cross-slab built into a roadside wall.

Glen of Aherlow, Tipperary (R 1913). At Ardane, in the south of the Glen of Aherlow, is the oval sacred enclosure called St Berechert's Kyle, which has two ancient crosses and over 50 cross-slabs set on the drystone walls.

Glendalough, Dublin (T 3119). The Vale of Glendalough contains many sacred remains associated with the sixth-century monastic settlement of St Kevin. They include St Kevin's Cross (*c.* 1150).

Inishcealtra (Holy Island), in Lough Derg, Clare (R 1618). The holy island of St Caimin has a circular enclosure with the Cross of Cathasach (*c.* 1094).

Inishkeen, Upper Loch Erne, Fermanagh (H 2233). 5 km (3 miles) southeast of Enniskillen is Inishkeen, where St Fergus's cemetery contains an antlered stone head of the Celtic pagan divinity called Cernunnos.

Inishtooskert, Blasket Islands, Kerry (Q 0210). This holy island has three stone crosses.

Kells (Ceanannas Mór), Meath (N 2727). In the market-place is a high cross on its original base. Among its carvings are several martial arts scenes, including quarterstaff fighting and wrestling. In the churchyard are crosses and a stone slab with an ancient sundial that shows the old northern European method of time-telling through the eight tides of the day. Close to the round tower is a high cross, with a Latin inscription, while next to the church is the unfinished cross that uniquely shows the stonemason's technique.

Kilfenora, Clare (R 1119). Here is an eleventh-century cross, which, with that at Dysert O'Dea (q.v.) is the most important example of the type in which a full-length figure of Christ is carved on the cross, transforming the Celtic Cross into a crucifix.

Killaloe, Limerick (R 1717). In the churchyard of St Flannan's Oratory is Thorgrim's Stone, dating from the first millennium, which is a cross-shaft bearing an inscription in both the runic and ogham scripts.

Kilmakedar, Kerry (Q 0411). A remarkable sundial-cross stands close to the Romanesque church. It is in the form of a wheel-headed cross with a flattened top, resembling some of the carved crosses at Clonmacnois.

Kilnasaggart, Louth (O 3031). Here there is an inscribed granite pillar dating from around the year 700.

Loughrea, Galway (M 1622). 6.5 km (4 miles) northeast of Loughrea is the Turoe Stone, a phallic-shaped *omphalos* with La Tène-style carvings.

Monasterboice, Louth (O 3028). The Celtic monastery founded by St Buithe has three ancient crosses. Muiredach's Cross (*c.* 923) is one of the most finely developed and executed Celtic Crosses in existence. It has a crucifix-sunwheel with 'world mountain' base and 'heavenly house' capstone. The North and West crosses are also particularly noteworthy, as is the pillar sundial which is also carved with a wheel-cross.

Moone, Kildare (N 2719). The Moone Cross stands in the grounds of Moone Abbey. It is over 5 m (16 ft) tall. Its base bears a crucifixion scene, while the sunwheel-head has a four-fold spiral pattern.

Nendrum, Down (J 3536). The tallest sundial-pillar in Ireland stands in the churchyard here. Rediscovered as fragments in the 1920s, it has been pieced together and re-erected.

Reask (Riasc), Kerry (Q 0310). The pillar-cross here is asymmetrically shaped, following the horizon, with the remains of a former drilled hole at the left.

St Mullins, Carlow (S 2713). 12 km (7½ miles) north of New Ross at the holy place of St Moling is a ninth-century high cross.

Stepaside, Dublin (O 3122). North of Stepaside Farm, below the Three Rocks Mountain, are Jamestown Holy Well and cross.

Tallaght, Dublin (O 3022). St Máel-Rúáin's Cross stands in the churchyard of St Maelruan's church.

Tara, Meath (N 2925). Tara of the Kings (Teamhair na Riogh), the ancient royal capital of Erin, has many features, including the pillar-stone called *Lia Fáil*, said to be the inauguration-stone of the High Kings of Ireland.

Tory Island, Donegal (B 1844). In the ruined monastery are many cross- and slab-fragments, including the famous cursing-stones.

Tuam, Galway (M 1425). This has a fine twelfth-century cross.

Tullylease, Cork (R 1311). The ruins of the monastery of Tullylease contain St Berechert's Well and the Berechtuine Stone, an eighth-century cross-slab sculpted with spiral and geometrical patterns.

Tynan, Armagh (H 2734). Tynan Abbey, west of Armagh, has four stone crosses, probably dating from the eighth century. The Village Cross and the Terrace Cross were taken in 1844 from Egish churchyard, while the Well Cross and Island Cross were brought to Tynan from Glenarb.

White Island, Lower Lough Erne, Fermanagh (H 2135). The ruined church on White Island contains seven sculpted stone images of Pagan and Christian figures.

BIBLIOGRAPHY

Allen, J. Romilly and Anderson, Joseph *The Early Christian Monuments of Scotland*. Forfar, The Pinkfoot Press, 1993.

Anwyl, Edward *Celtic Religion*. London, Constable, 1906.

Bächtold-Stäubli, Hanns (editor) *Handworterbuch des deutschen Aberglaubens*. 9 vols., Berlin, Walter De Gruyter, 1927–42.

Bailey, R. N. and Cramp, R. J. *Corpus of Anglo-Saxon Stone Sculpture, Vol. II, Cumberland, Westmoreland and Lancashire north-of-the-sands*. Oxford, Oxford University Press, 1988.

Bain, George *Celtic Art: The Methods of Construction*. Glasgow, McLellan, 1951.

Bamford, Christopher and Marsh, William Price *Celtic Christianity*. Edinburgh, Floris Books, 1986.

Baring-Gould, Sabine and Fisher, John *The Lives of the British Saints*, 4 vols. London, Honourable Society of Cymmrodorion, 1908.

Bauchhenss, Gerhard *Jupitergigantensäulen*. Aalen, Limesemuseum Aalen, 1976.

Benoit, F. *Le Symbolisme dans les sanctuaires de la Gaule*. Brussels, 1970.

Bittel, Kurt, Kimmig, Wolfgang and Schiek, Siegwalt (editors) *Die Kelten in Baden-Württemberg*. Stuttgart, 1981.

Bötticher, Carl *Der Baumkultus der Hellenen*. Berlin 1856.

Bowen, Dewi *Ancient Siluria, its old stones and ceremonial sites*. Felinfach, Llanerch, 1992.

Bowen, E. G. *The Settlements of the Celtic Saints in Wales*. Cardiff, University of Wales Press, 1956.

Bromwich, R. *Trioedd Ynys Prydein*. Cardiff, University of Wales Press, 1979.

Brunaux, Jean Louis *The Celtic Gauls: Gods, Rites and Sanctuaries*, London, Seaby, 1988.

Bryce, Derek *Symbolism of the Celtic Cross*. Llandyssul, Gomer, 1989.

Burgess, Frederick *English Churchyard Memorials*. London, Dent, 1963.

Campbell, J. G. *Superstitions of the Highlands and Islands of Scotland*. Edinburgh, 1900.

Campion, Nicholas *The Great Year: Astrology, Millenarianism and History in the Western Tradition*. London, Penguin Arkana, 1994.

Chadwick, Nora K. *The Age of the Saints in the Early Celtic Church*. London, Oxford University Press, 1963.

Close-Brooks, J. and Stevenson, R. B. K. *Dark Age Sculpture*. Edinburgh, RCHM, 1982.

Cramp, R. J. *Corpus of Anglo-Saxon Stone Sculpture, Vol. I. County Durham and Northumberland*. Oxford, Oxford University Press, 1984.

Crossing, William *The Ancient Stone Crosses of Dartmoor and its Borderland*. Exeter, 1902.

Cubbon, M. *The Art of Manx Crosses*. Douglas, The Manx Museum and National Trust, 1971.

Davies, Wendy *Wales in the Early Middle Ages*. Leicester, Leicester University Press, 1982.

Davis, Courtney *The Art of Celtia*. London, Blandford, 1993.

de Paor, Máire and Liam *Early Christian Ireland*. London, Thames and Hudson, 1958.

De Vries, Jan *Keltische Religion*. Stuttgart, Kohlhammer, 1961.

Dexter, T. H. *Old Cornish Crosses*. London, 1896.

Dillon, M. and Chadwick, N. K. *The Celtic Realms*. London, Cardinal, 1967.

Dunbar, J. G. and Fisher, I. *Iona*. London, HMSO, 1983.

Edwards, N. and Lane, A. *Early Medieval Settlements in Wales AD 400–1100*. Cardiff, Early Medieval Wales Research Group, 1988.

Ellis-Davidson, H. R. *Myths and Symbols in Pagan Europe*. Manchester, Manchester University Press, 1988.

Evans-Wentz, W. Y. *The Fairy Faith in Celtic Countries*, Oxford, Oxford University Press, 1911.

Filtzinger, Phillip *Hic saxa loquuntur*. Aalen, Limesmuseum Aalen, 1980.

Gantz, J. *Early Irish Myths and Sagas*. Harmondsworth, Penguin, 1981.

Gauthier, J. S. 'Les Croix Bretonnes.' *Bulletin de la Société Archéologique et Historique de Nantes*. 145–58, 1937.

Gelling, Peter and Davidson, Hilda Ellis *The Chariot of the Sun and Other Rites and Symbols of the Northern Bronze Age*. London, Aldine, 1969.

Green, M. J. *The Gods of the Celts*. Gloucester, Alan Sutton, 1986.

Grimm, J. L. (editor; translated by J. E. Stallybrass) *Teutonic Mythology*. 4 vols. London, 1880–88.

Grinsell, L. V. *Folklore of Prehistoric Sites in Britain*. Newton Abbot, David and Charles, 1976.

Halliday, W. R. *The Pagan Background of Early Christianity*. Liverpool, Hodder and Stoughton, 1925.

Hamlin, Ann *Historic Monuments of Northern Ireland*. Belfast, Department of the Environment, 1987.

Harbison, Peter *Pilgrimage in Ireland*. London, Barrie and Jenkins, 1991.

Hardings, Leslie *The Celtic Church in Britain*. London, 1972.

Henderson, G. *Survivals in Belief among the Celts*. Glasgow, James Maclehose, 1911.

Henderson, Isabel *The Picts*. London, Thames and Hudson, 1967.

—*The Art and Function of Rosemarkie's Pictish Monuments*. Rosemarkie, 1991.

Henken, Elissa R. *Tradition of the Welsh Saints*. Cambridge, Cambridge University Press, 1987.

Henry, Françoise *Irish High Crosses*. Dublin, 1964.

Herrmann, Paul *Das Altgermanische Priesterwesen*. Jena, Diderichs, 1929.

Jacobsthal, P. *Early Celtic Art*. Oxford, Oxford University Press, 1944.

Jones, David *Epoch and Artist*. London, Faber and Faber, 1959.

Jones, Prudence *Eight and Nine. Sacred numbers of Sun and Moon in the Pagan North*. Bar Hill, Fenris-Wolf, 1982.

—and Pennick, Nigel *A History of Pagan Europe*. London, Routledge, 1995.

Jung, Erich *Germanische Götter und Helden in christlicher Zeit*. Munich, J. F. Lehmanns Verlag, 1922.

Kaul, Flemming; Marazov, Ivan; Best, Jan and De Vries, Nanny *Thracian Tales on the Gundestrup Cauldron*. Amsterdam, Najade Press, 1991.

Kermode, P. M. C. and Herdmans, W. A. *Manks Antiquities*. Liverpool, 1914.

Laing, Gordon J. *Survivals of Roman Religion*. London, Harrap, 1931.

Laing, Lloyd and Jennifer *A Guide to the Dark Age Remains in Britain*. London, Constable, 1979.

Langdon, A. G. *Old Cornish Crosses*. Truro, 1896.

Leask, H. G. *Irish Churches and Monastic Buildings*. Dundalk, 1955.

Le Roux, Francoise and Guyonvarc'h, Christian-J. *Les druides*. Rennes, Ogam-Celticum, 1978.

Lewis, M. J. T. *Temples in Roman Britain*. Cambridge, Cambridge University Press, 1966.

MacAlister, R. A. S. *The Archaeology of Ireland*. London, 1928.

—*Corpus Inscriptionum Insularum Celticarum*. Dublin, 1945.

Mackenzie, W. M. *The Burghs of Scotland*. Edinburgh, 1948.

Mackey, James P. (editor) *An Introduction to Celtic Christianity*. Edinburgh, 1989.

MacManus, Dermot *The Middle Kingdom*. Gerrard's Cross, Colin Smythe, 1959.

McNeill, F. Marian *Iona. A History of the Island*. Glasgow, 1920.

Maringer, J. 'Priests and Priestesses in prehistoric Europe.' *History of Religions* 17(2), 101–120, 1977.

Marstrander, C. 'Thor en Irlande.' *Revue Celtique* 36, 1915–16.

Megaw, Ruth and Megaw, Vincent *Celtic Art*. London, Thames and Hudson, 1990.

Merne, John G. *A Handbook of Celtic Ornament*. Dublin, Mercier Educational, 1974.

Michell, John *The Old Stones of Land's End*. London, Garnstone Press, 1974.

Nash-Williams, V. E. *The Early Christian Monuments of Wales*. Cardiff, University of Wales Press, 1950.

Okasha, Elisabeth *Corpus of Early Christian Inscribed Stones of South-West Britain*. Leicester, Leicester University Press, 1993.

O'Rahilly, T. F. *Early Irish History and Mythology*, Dublin, Institute for Advanced Studies, 1946.

O'Riordain, S. P. 'The Genesis of the Celtic Cross.' In Penders (editor) *Feilscribhinn Torna*. Cork, 1947.

Pauli, L. *Keltischer Volksglaube. Amulette und sonderbestattungen am Durnberg*. Munich, 1975.

Pennick, Nigel *The Ancient Science of Geomancy*. London, Thames and Hudson, 1979.

—*Einst War Uns Die Erde Heilig*. Waldeck-Dehringhausen, Felicitas-Hübner Verlag, 1987.

—*Celtic Art in the Northern Tradition*. Bar Hill, Nideck, 1992.

— *Anima Loci*. Bar Hill, Nideck, 1993.

— *The Oracle of Geomancy*. Chieveley, Capall Bann, 1995.

— *Secret Signs, Symbols and Sigils*, Chieveley, Capall Bann, 1996.

—*Celtic Sacred Landscapes*. London, Thames and Hudson, 1996.

Radford, C. A. R. *Margam Stones Museum*. London, RCHM, 1949.

— and Donaldson, G. *Whithorn*. London, HMSO, 1984.

Redknap, Mark *The Christian Celts. Treasures of Late Celtic Wales*. Cardiff, National Museum of Wales, 1991.

Rees, Alwyn and Rees, Brinley *Celtic Heritage*. London, Thames and Hudson, 1967.

Rhys, John *Celtic Folklore*. Oxford, Oxford University Press, 1901.

Richardson, Hilary and Scarry, John *An Introduction to Irish High Crosses*, Cork, Mercier, 1990.

Rimmer, Alfred *Ancient Stone Crosses of England*. London, Virtue and Co., 1875.

Roe, Helen *The High Crosses of Kells*. Dublin, County Louth Archaeological and Historical Society, 1981.

Ross, Anne *Pagan Celtic Britain*. London, Constable, 1992.

Saintyves, P. *Corpus de Folklore Préhistorique en France et dans les Colonies Francaises*, 3 vols. Paris, 1934–36.

Seaborne, Malcolm *Celtic Crosses of Britain and Ireland*. Aylesbury, Shire Archaeology, 1994.

Simpson, W. Douglas *The Ancient Stones of Scotland*. London, Hale, 1973.

Smyth, Alfred P. *Warlords and Holy Men*. Edinburgh, 1989.

Stuart, John *Sculptured Stones of Scotland*. Aberdeen, 1856.

Sutherland, Elizabeth *In Search of the Picts*. London, 1994.

Thevenot, E. *Divinités et sanctuaires de la Gaule*. Paris, 1968.

Thomas, Charles *Christianity in Roman Britain to AD 500*. London, Thames and Hudson, 1981.

Thomas, Patrick *The Opened Door. A Celtic Spirituality*. Llandysul, Gomer, 1990.

— *A Candle in the Darkness, Celtic Spirituality from Wales*. Llandysul, Gomer, 1993.

Watkins, Alfred *The Old Standing Crosses of Herefordshire*. London, Simpkin Marshall, 1923.

Williams, Edward (editor) *Barddas*. Llandovery, Welsh Manuscripts Society, 1862.

Wirth, Hermann *Die Helige Urschrift der Menschheit*. 9 vols. Leipzig, Kohler und Amerlang, 1932–36.

Wood-Martin, W. G. *Pagan Ireland*. London, 1895.

—*Traces of the Elder Faiths of Ireland*. London, 1902.

Woodwark, T. H. *The Crosses on the North York Moors*. Whitby, 1924.

INDEX